# Keeping Minds Happy and Hea

*Keeping Minds Happy and Healthy* is a practical resource for teachers and shows how pupils can achieve and maintain excellent mental health. It focuses on identifying the main causes of unhappiness, stress and anxiety, by examining the difficulties a school system can inadvertently create for pupils. By developing resilience, empathic behaviour, social skills and self-respect during childhood, pupils will be better equipped to withstand the pressures of modern society and growing up.

With practical tip sheets and advice, *Keeping Minds Happy and Healthy* suggests ways to create a more positive educational experience for all pupils. Pat Guy shows how schools can increase all pupils' well-being, enabling them to deal with the challenging situations they face as they move through education and into the adult world.

**Pat Guy** is currently teaching in Eton College's Learning Centre, UK, and has previously published *Transforming Reading Skills in the Secondary School* with Routledge.

# Keeping Minds Happy and Healthy

## A handbook for teachers

Pat Guy

Routledge
Taylor & Francis Group

LONDON AND NEW YORK

First published 2017
by Routledge
2 Park Square, Milton Park, Abingdon, Oxon OX14 4RN

and by Routledge
711 Third Avenue, New York, NY 10017

*Routledge is an imprint of the Taylor & Francis Group, an informa business*

*British Library Cataloguing in Publication Data*
A catalogue record for this book is available from the British Library

*Library of Congress Cataloging in Publication Data*
Names: Guy, Pat, author.Title: Keeping minds happy and healthy : a
handbook for teachers / Pat Guy.Description: Abingdon, Oxon ; New York, NY
: Routledge is an imprint of the Taylor & Francis Group, an Informa Business,
[2017]Identifiers: LCCN 2016005952 | ISBN 9781138672505 (hardback)
| ISBN 9781138672512 (pbk.) | ISBN 9781315562483 (ebook)Subjects:
LCSH: Students--Mental health--Handbooks, manuals, etc. | Educational
psychology--Handbooks, manuals, ec.Classification: LCC LB3430 .G89 2017 |
DDC 371.7/13--dc23LC record available at https://lccn.loc.gov/2016005952

ISBN: 978-1-138-67250-5 (hbk)
ISBN: 978-1-138-67251-2 (pbk)
ISBN: 978-1-315-56248-3 (ebk)

Typeset in Melior
by GreenGate Publishing Services, Tonbridge, Kent

For Holly, Amy, Toby, Ruby, Jamie and Theo

# Contents

Contents

# Abbreviations

| | |
|---|---|
| ADD | attention deficit disorder |
| ADHD | attention deficit hyperactivity disorder |
| CAF | Consider All Factors |
| CAMH | Child and Adolescent Mental Health |
| CASE | Cognitive Acceleration through Science Education |
| CBI | Confederation of British Industry |
| CoRT | Cognitive Research Trust |
| IQ | intelligent quotient |
| KS2 | Key Stage 2 |
| NUT | National Union of Teachers |
| OECD | Organisation for Economic Co-operation and Development |
| PISA | Programme for International Student Assessment |
| PMI | Pluses, Minuses and Interesting factors |
| PPE | Politics, Philosophy and Economics |
| PSHE | Personal, Social, Health and Economic education |
| SATs | Standard Assessment Tests |
| SEN | special educational needs |
| SpLD | Specific Learning Difficulty |
| SSP | School Sport Partnerships |

# The need for an inclusive education system that embraces and builds on pupil difference

*This didn't come to me through academic reading or study. It came to me through seeing apartheid and its impact on the people whom I had responsibility for as a priest.*

(Trevor Huddlestone, religious and political activist)

Over recent years, concerns relating to the rise of mental health problems among children and young people of school age have increased. Discussions on the most appropriate support for pupils appear to focus on increased input at points of crisis, when the child's or young person's anxiety becomes obvious, perhaps through the improvement of links between schools and Child and Adolescent Mental Health (CAMH), counselling services or anti-bullying groups. However, if appropriate support could be given to pupils throughout their education, much of the unhappiness that seems to be part of modern childhood might be avoided. If schools could increase all pupils' well-being, they might be better prepared for the challenging situations they will inevitably face as they move through school and into the adult world. By developing resilience, empathic behaviour, social skills and self-respect during childhood, pupils will be better equipped to withstand the negative pressures of modern society.

In order for this to happen, the education system needs to directly and actively promote pupils' mental well-being, both to secure the emotional health of the general population and also to enable society to benefit from the diverse range of talents and skills of the population. 'There is too narrow a focus on school outcomes, with a neglect

1

of the vocational as well as the wider development of interests and attitudes essential for a contributing and personally fulfilling life' (Sir Tim Brighouse 2015).

Society must adopt an approach towards education that is accepting of individual difference to enable pupils to move into adulthood as secure and confident individuals. An increased breadth of educational outcomes would benefit both the individual and society. The current educational system is over academically prescriptive and confuses the ability to perform well in examinations with intelligent behaviour. To succeed in life, an individual's attitudes will be as important as their academic achievement. A pupil may excel in exams yet be unmotivated, have creative flair yet lack confidence, be academically able yet be awkward in social situations, be mathematically talented yet over anxious. If every young person is to maximise their potential, the curriculum must include opportunities to develop positive attitudes and strength of character. Exam qualifications will get the job interview, but other attributes will secure the job, with success in an interview a beginning rather than a final result. While at work, young people will need to collaborate with colleagues, be conscientious, manage unpleasant peers and awkward situations, resist the temptation to call in sick unnecessarily, cope when things go wrong, follow instructions from superiors, control their emotions, while simultaneously dealing with personal issues: relationships, family life, managing finances and maintaining their health.

How would the current system change if every pupil were destined to be an entrepreneur or self-employed? What should be taught in schools to prepare pupils for a future that cannot be envisaged? Currently the examination system is used to select and sort individuals for their future role in society, but how can we be certain of the specific skills adults will need in ten, twenty or fifty years time?

As a result of the emphasis placed on exam qualifications, many pupils have an unrealistic expectation of their potential after leaving school. Teachers are able to teach to the exam in a way that favours those pupils who learn facts presented in a structured, sequential manner, while others who prefer a more active or practical approach to learning are disadvantaged. As a result, some pupils will over-perform and others will under-perform in terms of their potential for future success.

> **Key point**
>
> Exams measure an individual's ability to take exams.

Very few successful artists, athletes, musicians or actors will have an A* in Art, Sports Studies, Music or Drama 'A' Levels. When a pupil passes twelve GCSEs with top grades, this does not indicate an in-depth knowledge and interest in those subjects, but rather an in-depth knowledge of how to pass exams. Exams are not designed to identify individual talent but rather pupils' ability to memorise and regurgitate syllabus content in a prescribed manner. Countless individuals have gone on to be successful in their chosen field with few formal qualifications: Alan Sugar, Elton John, Joss Stone, Walt Disney, Erin Brockovich, Steve Redgrave, Richard Branson, Zoe Wanamaker, David Beckham, Jennifer Aniston, John Major, Toyah Willcox, Ozzy Osbourne and Guy Ritchie. Significant numbers of high achievers were considered to have learning difficulties or destined for failure at school, while many of those considered to be high flyers at school failed to fulfil their apparent potential in adult life.

## The school reports of a few successful adults

*Sue Perkins (broadcaster):* 'What Sue lacks in intelligence, she makes up for in stupidity.'

*Eric Morecambe (comedian):* 'I hate to say this, but Eric will never get anywhere in life.'

*Beryl Bainbridge (novelist):* 'Though her written work is the product of an obviously lively imagination, it is a pity that her spelling derives from the same source. Her knowledge of Geography is so poor as to make one wonder if she is simple minded.'

*Dame Judi Dench (actress):* 'Judi would be a very good pupil if she lived in this world.'

*Winston Churchill (politician):* 'He is so regular in his irregularity that I really don't know what to do.'

*John Lennon (musician):* 'Certainly on the road to failure … hopeless … rather a clown in class … wasting other pupils' time.'

*Stephen Fry (comedian, playwright and novelist):* 'He has glaring faults and they have certainly glared at us this term. English: Bottom, rightly.'

*Charles Darwin (scientist):* 'I was considered by all my masters and my father a very ordinary boy, rather below the common standard of intellect.'

*Thomas Edison (businessman and inventor):* 'Edison's mind wandered so much in school that his teacher referred to him as being "addled".'

*Jilly Cooper (novelist):* 'Jilly has set herself an extremely low standard which she has failed to maintain.'

*Roy Hudd (entertainer):* 'Has a ragbag mind stuffed with information of no possible interest to anyone but himself.'

*Peter Ustinov (actor, director, playwright):* 'Shows great originality, which must be curbed at all costs.'

# Reference

Brighouse, T. (2015) We have much to learn from the spirit of '45. *Times Educational Supplement*, 27 March.

# CHAPTER 1

# Pupils' experience of education

## Aspects of the current education system that can demoralise pupils

There are aspects of the current educational system that demoralise pupils and add unnecessary stress and pressure to their lives. This chapter will explore five negative aspects of pupils' school experience: the development of unhelpful mindsets that serve to undermine children's self-confidence, the apparent preference for extrovert behaviour over quiet and thoughtful behaviour, a failure to acknowledge the variety of children's learning styles, a lack of appreciation of the impact of chronological age on performance, and the overuse of testing. These aspects do not stand alone but are closely interrelated.

It is within the power of all schools to reduce the impact of such practices and to extend the breadth of provision they are able to offer their pupils.

## The development of unhelpful mindsets

Carol Dweck (2006) of Stanford University has identified two types of 'mindset' that individuals can possess: a fixed or a growth mindset. Young people with a fixed mindset believe their ability levels are set at birth, therefore performance in school is predetermined and their ability, or lack of ability, is a genetic trait that they can do nothing about. Other pupils will possess a growth mindset, believing they can improve their attainment through persistence and hard work.

Unfortunately the current education system predisposes children towards the development of a fixed mindset through, for example, the introduction of formal teaching approaches in Key Stage 1 when children are too young to cope with such methods. The children may be developmentally incapable of paying attention, producing neat work, spelling key words or recognising phonic blends and so are set up to fail and consider themselves to be stupid. Belief in a fixed mindset will be perpetuated when secondary schools focus on exam results, encouraging pupils to perceive themselves purely in terms of exam success or failure. Intelligent pupils are good at exams and tests, therefore pupils who get poor results in exams and tests are not intelligent.

Dweck believes that when pupils possess a fixed mindset and consistently compare their performance with others, or are compared unfavourably to supposedly high achievers, their levels of motivation in school will decline.

Watkins (2010) makes a similar distinction between pupils' attitudes to academic work, referring to fixed and growth mindsets as performance orientation and learning orientation. In performance orientation, pupils believe that ability equals success, leading to negative self-evaluation when a task proves difficult. In learning orientation, pupils believe that effort leads to success, that everyone can improve and that personal satisfaction will increase when a difficult task is accomplished.

Possessing a fixed mindset can affect individuals in different ways. Pupils who see themselves as failures in school will assume that they were born stupid and are powerless to improve. They will become disillusioned when faced with work they do not immediately understand, and imagine that collaborating with others or being observed working problems out in a steady, methodical way will provide further evidence of their slow mind. Some pupils may be tempted to take shortcuts and cheat rather than be seen to be struggling. Cheating will have implications for their future learning as new information will need to be built on their prior understanding. Some of these pupils will withdraw and dismiss school as being 'boring'. Others will channel their frustration into sabotaging those situations that make them feel uncomfortable, creating problems for staff and peers.

Those who have been told they are intelligent may have private concerns that they are not worthy of the high-ability label and be unwilling to challenge themselves, experiment or collaborate with others in case they are seen to fall short of expectations. Some of these pupils will become aggressive in defence of their intellect.

Children with fixed mindsets become adults with fixed mindsets and will take their attitudes into their future careers and adult life.

In February 2011, a judicial review deemed Michael Gove's decision as Secretary of State for Education to axe 'Building Schools for the Future' projects in six local authority areas to be unlawful, as he had failed to consult before imposing the cuts. Many politicians have limited knowledge of education or child development, but believe themselves capable of taking decisions that have long-lasting effects on schools. When politicians have fixed mindsets and feel that they are part of an intellectual elite, they will not always appreciate the wisdom of consulting those with specialist knowledge and experience and listening to and considering their advice. In March 2013, some 100 academics warned of the dangers posed by Michael Gove's new National Curriculum. Gove, an English graduate from Lady Margaret Hall, Oxford, retorted that the critics were 'Marxist' and 'Enemies of Promise', that 'there is good academia and bad academia'.

## Extroverts v introverts

Society benefits from having a range of talents at its disposal, but educational approaches in Western countries tend to favour the extrovert in the classroom. When introverts are not recognised and valued in school, the message is given to children and young people that extrovert behaviour is the desirable norm. This assumption will follow introverted pupils through school, sapping the confidence of quieter, more thoughtful children. The contribution made by different personality types must be recognised in schools to ensure young people move into the adult world valuing the skills that different individuals bring to a situation.

The danger exists that extroverts with exam ability and fixed mindsets will thrive and dominate major walks of life. While some cultures admire outgoing, chatty, self-confident types, other cultures see quiet thoughtfulness as preferable. Eastern philosophers would see self-promotion and over-confidence as a deplorable personality trait and would consider introverts more likely to think things through carefully before speaking, observing and listening rather than promoting their own interests. Reflective individuals will tend to listen more than talk, think before speaking and may express themselves better in writing than in conversation. It is often observed that those pupils who talk most in the classroom think least. As Plato said: 'Wise men talk because they have something to say; fools talk to say something.'

The Indian political campaigner Mahatma Gandhi believed restraint to be one of his greatest assets.

> I have naturally formed the habit of restraining my thoughts. A thoughtless word hardly ever escaped my tongue or pen. Experience has taught me that silence is part of the spiritual discipline of a votary of truth. We find so many people impatient to talk. All this talking can hardly be said to be of any benefit to the world. It is so much waste of time [sic]. My shyness has been in reality my shield and buckler. It has allowed me to grow. It has helped me in my discernment of truth.

Extroverts with a fixed mindset believe they command respect by being confident and decisive. They enjoy verbal battles and scoring points over others in arguments, seeing such victories as a further demonstration of their intelligence. In many discussions, the point of the argument can be lost in the excitement of defeating the opponent.

On 17 April 2014, John Bercow, Speaker of the House of Commons, reported that the 'histrionics and cacophony of noise' in Prime Minister's Question Time were so bad that a number of experienced female MPs had told him they would stop attending.

The charity The Daedalus Trust lists fifteen features of hubris or excessive pride and self-confidence in individuals. These include dangerous attributes that can been seen in many who hold positions of authority: an excessive confidence in their own opinion combined with a contempt for the opinions of others, an interest in self-glorification that enables them to act solely to enhance their own standing and be blind to any unfavourable outcomes of their decisions.

Narcissus extroverts with fixed mindsets will have a positive self-image, high levels of confidence and view themselves to be capable of taking control. These powerful individuals will choose similar 'strong and decisive' personalities to work with. Such personality traits could be considered to be male, and may go some way to explaining the glass ceiling that exists for women in those professions and businesses that are the traditional strongholds of men.

Research in America by Leslie *et al.* (2015) suggests that attitudes similar to those prevalent in the business world extend into academia. Their research involved polling scholars from fifty different academic fields about the necessity for talent, as opposed to discipline and hard work, for success in their specific subject. Results from the poll showed that those disciplines where inborn genius was valued over hard work and dedication had fewer women and African-Americans earning PhDs. These fields included Maths and Science (Physics and Chemistry) in addition to some of the social sciences, including Economics and Philosophy.

In September 2014, it was announced that Veronique Laury was to join the ranks of the five female CEOs of FTSE 100 companies. In the US, twenty-three of the Fortune 500 companies have a female chief executive. Progress in equal opportunities is more likely to occur when the habit of 'like hiring like' changes to enable the development and promotion of a more diverse pool of employees.

Malcolm Gladwell (2002) introduced the concept of the Talent Myth. Gladwell felt that inappropriate promotions are often made in business with some employees placed in positions they should not hold, while worthier employees are kept from rising up through the hierarchy. Extrovert personalities are most likely to climb the promotion ladder with their confident presentation skills masking lesser qualities. However, individuals who are good listeners may be better for business than those interested in self-promotion. Narcissistic personalities are less likely to consult others, more likely to take credit for achievements and less likely to accept blame for failure. They will expect to be able to complete tasks quickly and easily and so may be in danger of making far-reaching decisions that are inadequately thought through. They will defend their decisions vehemently and see any criticism as a personal affront. According to Cain (2012): 'The archetypical extrovert prefers action to contemplation, risk taking to heed-taking, certainty to doubt. He favours quick decisions, even at the risk of being wrong.'

Ongoing research by Delaney *et al.* (2006) into the mindsets of large, influential American companies found that employees recognised and appreciated the positive aspects of working for companies with a growth mindset, but reported that in companies with a fixed mindset, fellow employees 'engage in more devious practices – keeping secrets, hoarding information – all designed to make them look like winners in the talent hierarchy'. Unfortunately such attitudes do not promote creative or collaborative problem solving.

The main advice given to the parents of a quiet child at a school Parents' Evening will relate to encouraging them to participate more in class, contribute to discussions and try to overcome their 'shyness'. Many introverted pupils are late bloomers, not realising their potential at school because of the way in which the classroom environment favours the gregarious, verbally dominant pupil. Once an adult, quiet individuals can choose their workplace, where they live, who they live with, what they do in their free time and be happy in situations they select specifically to meet their needs and interests. It is then that introverts will begin to shine. No one should be made to feel uncomfortable or inadequate in school because they are thoughtful or self-contained. Society needs to value diversity: both extroverts and introverts must be allowed to contribute in their own way to ensure a well-balanced approach to decision making in all sectors of the community.

> **Key point**
>
> In order to create a balanced society, extroverts with exam ability and fixed mindsets must not be allowed to dominate in the classroom. It is not a question of being superior or inferior, but finding strength in difference.

## A failure to recognise and provide for pupils with alternative approaches to learning

> If all children are taught the same things in the same way, only some will have the chance to excel. The UK's one-size-fits-all school system, with a national curriculum intended to minimise inequalities of opportunity, may inadvertently be favouring a subset of children.
>
> (Bond 2014: 30)

Everyone involved in the education of children will be aware of their different rates of developmental progress and of the wide range of normal childhood behaviours. While there will always be some pupils with additional needs who require specialist forms of teaching, there will be many other children whose personality type, levels of maturity or developmental stage are towards the ends of an average spectrum. Children are all individuals and their differences need to be taken into account in educational provision. The National Curriculum puts emphasis on teachers covering curriculum content. If the lessons designated for a specific topic have been completed, yet pupil knowledge is still insecure, there is not always time for revision. The curriculum content must be covered, although this does not necessarily involve all pupils learning. There is a danger that, with the curriculum narrowing and lessons becoming increasingly exam focused, the range of children's learning styles and differing rates of development will not be acknowledged and more pupils' needs will be left unmet. Increasing numbers of children are diagnosed as having learning difficulties when they just find it difficult to conform to a system that is not child friendly. They are square pegs forced into round holes.

It is quite normal for children to be more energetic and active than adults. However, between 2000 and 2010, worldwide prescriptions for Ritalin, a drug used to combat the effects of attention deficit, doubled. The increase in Ritalin prescriptions for children and young people in the UK seems to mirror that of the USA, where there was an 83 per cent increase in sales of the drug between 2006 and 2010. The symptoms of ADHD (attention deficit hyperactivity disorder) have been shown to be reduced when children have regular access to outdoor play. Outdoor play gives children the opportunity to move freely in unrestricted open areas, to be noisy, burn off energy, get messy and use all of their senses. Unfortunately, not all schools are able to provide opportunities for adequate exercise and physical activity. Pupils in the independent sector spend on average five hours or more a week participating in sport, while pupils in the state sector spend on average less than two hours a week on sporting activities.

Active play in gardens, parks and on the street has been replaced for a significant number of children by entertainment within the home: television, the internet, social media sites and computer games. If children's need for physical exercise were recognised, more opportunities could be provided for them to use their energy, to play in the park on the way home from school, to cycle to friends' houses, to play in the garden or street or join local sports clubs. Many schools have added inadvertently to the problem by reducing the time dedicated to play during lunch hours and cutting an afternoon playtime for all but the youngest pupils. The reasons given for this include the pressure of an overloaded curriculum and the fact that some of the children have little idea of how to play and will get bored. Boredom has long been acknowledged as a way to energise children into devising their own games.

Society should recognise the value of variety and the contribution that pupils with different skills can make. Individuals with ADHD have energy and are risk takers. Individuals with Asperger's syndrome are valuable to society because of their eye for detail and ability to focus. Dyslexics are useful to society for their alternative problem-solving skills. Schools need to cater for and encourage such diversity.

According to Milne (2000): 'Brains that work differently are here for a reason. They give us different operating systems that solve problems in different ways. Everyone can benefit from their creativity.' Barber (2015) adds: 'Across history, the age-old struggle between marauding nomads and static defensive farmers shows that innovation comes mostly from those who roam outside civilised space.'

> Instead of capturing my energy, nurturing it and channelling it into something positive, a lot of the teachers tried to subdue it, fearing it might be dangerous. Mrs St Johnson never did that. She allowed me to be me and recognised that I was capable of learning, given the right circumstances.
>
> (Amanda Donohoe, actress, ADHD)

> People need to think about systems that could help Asperger's people – not helping them to fit in, but helping them to be happy and thrive. I think forcing them to be normal is the worst possible thing.
>
> (Daniel Lightwing, International Mathematical
> Olympiad medallist, Asperger adult)

Many successful individuals have an element of obsession in their personality that gives them an edge over individuals who are merely interested in their hobby or career. Pupils with Asperger's syndrome are known for their obsessive behaviour and, when such individuals are able to turn their interests into careers, many will achieve success because of the amount of time they are prepared to dedicate to their work. Most top athletes would admit to possessing an obsessive trait.

> My utter absorption in surfing had no rational content. It simply compelled me; there was a deep mine of beauty and wonder in it.
>
> (William Finnegan, journalist and author)

It is no coincidence that obsessive behaviour, focus and task commitment are frequently recorded as personality traits of successful people. Society could support and benefit from such talented individuals rather than focusing on any perceived short comings.

Psychologist Kazimierz Dabrowski (1972) suggested that gifted children experience 'overexcitabilities' that include imaginational (day dreaming), psychomotor (surplus nervous energy or being too active to pay attention to detail), intellectual (challenging authority and concentrating obsessively), sensory (excessive aversion to or attachment to lights, sounds and smells) and mental (compassion, shyness, anxiety). The personality traits of gifted children as described by Dabrowski are all aspects of what could be alternatively defined as specific learning difficulties: attention deficit disorder (ADD), ADHD, Asperger's syndrome and sensory perception disorders.

All childhood behaviours are open to interpretation according to the context in which the child is placed. Surplus energy would be a plus for pupils competing in a demanding netball, hockey, football or tennis match, but not in a 'chalk and talk' lesson. Obsessive concentration would be considered a skill except when a thirty-five-minute lesson timetable is in place.

> I must have taken tens of thousands, maybe hundreds of thousands of free kicks. I would go to the local park, place the ball on the ground and aim at the wire meshing over the window of a small community hut. When my dad got home from work, we would go over to the goalposts together. He would stand between me and the goal, forcing me to bend the ball around him. People looking on must have thought we were mad. We kept going even when the sun had gone down, playing by the light coming out of the windows of the houses that surrounded the park.
>
> (David Beckham, former England international footballer)

Statistical research carried out by Logan (2009) shows that dyslexia is relatively common among business entrepreneurs: Richard Branson, Anita Roddick, Theo Paphitis, Sophie Conran, Henry Ford, Peter Stringfellow and Lord Sugar. Logan suggests several reasons for this. Dyslexics tend to think differently and will be able to see the big picture in a business plan. They are happy to delegate as they will be aware of the need to compensate for personal shortcomings, are likely to have well-developed oral skills and will prefer to work in their own, perhaps idiosyncratic, style rather than conform to traditional ways of working.

Dyslexia certainly makes you more resourceful and makes you think in different ways. I come across a problem and I circumnavigate it and take a different route.

(Sophie Conran, business woman, dyslexic)

While their academic peers are collecting academic qualifications, dyslexic pupils will be learning lessons. When supported appropriately and sensitively in school, dyslexic pupils will develop essential life skills: a sense of humour, a work ethic, alternative problem-solving approaches and the ability to bounce back from disappointment.

For information relating to specific learning differences, see Section IV, 'Specific learning difficulties or differences'.

## The failure to recognise the effect of chronological age on pupil performance

According to Geake (2009): 'Brain development is driven by life experiences, rather than chronological age and children's learning needs are best addressed by having them engage in a curriculum that is appropriate for their stage of learning readiness, largely independent of their birthday.'

In the mid-twentieth century, the French developmental psychologist Jean Piaget formulated a theory of cognitive development based on the developmental stages through which all children pass. According to this theory, children cannot grasp concepts until they have reached the appropriate stage of development and teaching a child a skill before they are cognitively ready will be unsuccessful.

I am 42 this month, but I am still brought up short by the English language, even though my parents were English teachers and I make a living from trying to string sentences together. My five-year-old's homework last week left me grappling for Google, as she was asked to write sentences using 'fronted adverbials'. At first, I thought this meant some kind of ornate porch. After a while, I realised it was part of the more rigorous curriculum.

(Jane Merrick, journalist)

Children are not automatons and their development cannot be speeded up. Children are naturally programmed to explore and learn to control their environment at their own pace. If they are not taught in an age-appropriate way, they will soon lose interest in an activity. If they are asked to do something beyond their developmental stage, they will fail. If they fail enough times, they will lose confidence and be reluctant to attempt new activities.

> ### Key point
> The current education system holds significant responsibility for the development of the fixed mindset that schools will try to eliminate at some later stage.

Research into brain function shows that the development of the conductive material of neurons in the brain follows different patterns in different individuals and the maturation of the areas required for reading, for example, is not completed until between five and seven years of age. To attempt to teach a child to read before they are ready will be counter-productive and demonstrates an ignorance of their long-term needs. Many children are not mature enough to learn to read when they start school and so will be set up to fail. Reading is a skill that is too important for the child's academic success and self-esteem for this to be allowed to happen. When children are pushed to develop decoding skills before they are ready, reading will appear to be yet one more boring and difficult chore to be endured in school. Children will be less likely to read for pleasure and their reading skills will remain underdeveloped.

> From the moment children in England enter the reception class, the pressure is on for them to learn to read, write and do formal written maths. In many schools, children are identified as 'behind' with reading before they would even have started school in other countries. There is no research evidence to support claims from the government that 'earlier is better'.
>
> (Whitebread 2012)

It does not matter how slowly you go as long as you do not stop.

(Confucius 551–479 BC)

Legally children are not required to start school until the term after their fifth birthday. Individual headteachers and councils can create unnecessary stress for families by insisting summer born children whose parents delay their children's school entry miss out their reception year and go straight into Year 1. Decisions about admission to school need to be made in the interests of the individual child and not for administrative ease. The chronological age of summer born children and the long-term implications of their relative immaturity need to be carefully considered. Some 45 per cent of young footballers in Premier League academies in 2014 were born at the beginning of the school year in September, October and November, and 10 per cent were born at the end of the school year in June, July and August. Boys born at the beginning of the school year will be more physically mature than those born at the end of the school year: they will be taller, stronger and faster. Such players will be chosen to play for class, school and club teams and get more practice, better coaching and be involved in more matches. The advantages of physical maturity in school sport are easy to understand but differences in intellectual maturity may be less apparent. It is essential to consider the effect of a child's birth date on their academic development.

> Children born in August are more likely to be considered to have special educational needs than their peers by the end of primary school. Fifteen thousand eleven year olds born in August were classified as having SEN in 2013 compared to ten thousand eleven year olds with birthdays in September.
>
> (DfE 2010)

Twenty years ago, pupils with birthdays at the beginning of September would have started secondary school close to their twelfth birthday, while children with a birthday in late August would start just after their eleventh birthday. It has always been the case that some children would have a full year longer in primary school than others. However, staggered entry into the Reception class, in addition to a later leap-frogging of the school year in Year 3 or Year 4 when the child had established basic literacy and numeracy skills, helped to reduce the impact of chronological age on pupil self-esteem.

Children born in the summer months have always been at a disadvantage, but changes in the age at which children start school and the pressure on schools to introduce formal learning at an earlier stage have aggravated the problem. Today, a pupil may start in a reception class in the week following their fourth birthday and be physically incapable of sitting still, following instructions, listening for any period of time or learning through formal approaches. This will not be through any shortcoming of the child, but a question of physical and mental maturity over which the child has no control.

Research by Norbury *et al.* (2015) suggests that children with summer birthdays drop behind quickly in their reception year because they do not have the language skills necessary to meet curriculum targets, not because of any specific language weakness but as a result of their relative immaturity.

> Explanations for the higher prevalence of Special Educational Needs (SEN) in summer-born children include stress experienced as a result of early failure generating lower self-esteem and expectations for younger pupils, and failure of teachers to make sufficient allowance for relative age in their assessments of educational need; these reasons are inextricably linked to the general trend of lower attainment compared with older peers.
>
> (DfE 2010)

## The overuse of testing

The current educational system requires continual testing of the development of pupils' academic skills. This need to relate input to outcome and monitor progress has meant increased and regular assessment.

The use of repeated practice tests impresses on pupils the importance of the tests. It encourages them to adopt test-taking strategies designed to avoid effort and responsibility. Repeated practice tests are, therefore, detrimental to higher order thinking.

(Assessment Reform Group 2002)

Youngsters are starting to feel anxious about performing at school – tests and SATs and the risk of it all. Teachers are under such enormous pressure to show progress at an individual level, pupil by pupil, week by week.

(Schools and Students Health Education Unit 2015)

The Government needs to consider seriously the impact of their policies on children's well-being. Children can now expect to be branded 'failures' when barely into primary education, and many of those who undergo high-stakes tests and examinations at all stages of school life experience serious stress-related anxiety.

(Kevin Courtney, Deputy General Secretary of the
National Union of Teachers)

Children who fail their end of Key Stage 2 (KS2) Standard Assessment Tests (SATs) in English and Maths (failure to achieve a Level 4) will retake the tests in their first year of secondary school to ensure there is 'zero tolerance of failure and mediocrity'. The original National Curriculum stated that Level 4 was the average attainment of pupils at the end of Year 6. It was not a question of a test that a child passed or failed, but a measure of an *average* level of achievement.

I suppose one of the biggest failures in our educational system is the large number of people who have no comprehension at all of what the term average might actually mean. When the first national tests were given to seven year olds roughly 50 per cent scored at Level 3, the supposed 'average', and 25 per cent at each of Levels 1 and 3. It was the sort of distribution you would expect.

(Wragg 1998)

Secondary schools must show that at least 80 per cent of children who 'fail' their KS2 SATs in Year 6 have passed their re-sits. This will hold implications for the 25 per cent of pupils who do not reach the expected level at the end of KS2. The period of transition from primary to secondary school is a difficult time for many children, and re-testing will only add to the pressure they feel. An acceptable level of achievement in SATs at the end of KS2 will become even more important and, when so much is at stake for schools, inevitably rote learning and cramming will dominate teaching in the last years of KS2.

There will be no new start for pupils who fail to make the grade, just recognition of previous failure. Exam-focused coaching for the 100,000 children who fail to meet KS2 targets will be essential during their first terms at secondary school. Schools will appreciate that this is inappropriate educationally, but be powerless in the face of government directives. Some pupils are unlikely to be welcomed into schools, as leadership teams will be aware that if the children underperform, the school will face government intervention with school leaders' jobs threatened.

As well as additional testing at the beginning of secondary school, national testing will be in place for four and five year olds. The tests will take place in the first few weeks of school, when most of the children are below compulsory school age. The children's 'baseline' ability in literacy, reasoning and cognition will be assessed. The fact that the testing occurs at the beginning of the Autumn Term will be additionally problematic for children born in the summer. They may have started reception classes a few days after their fourth birthday and are likely to struggle when compared with children who are a whole calendar year older. There is a danger that such early assessment when some children will have only just learnt to talk in complete sentences will define the younger children in the class as 'red table' material until proven otherwise.

As it is recognised that the younger the child when tested, the lower the correlation with their subsequent performance, early assessment would seem an unnecessary risk to take with children's self-esteem.

The experience of starting school will provoke similar feelings in the child as when an adult starts a new job. Will anyone like me? Will someone dislike me? What will I have to eat for lunch? Will I be able to do everything? Where are the toilets? It is essential for pupils' well-being that their first few weeks in school focus on settling and reassuring rather than provoking anxiety. They should achieve easy success in all tasks and not be made to feel inadequate in any way, but led to assume their future will be golden and that school is a good place to be.

> ### Key point
>
> It is important to remember that children entering Reception classes are four years old.

Four year olds will perform differently in assessments for many reasons and they may be assessed as above average, average or below average within the same week or even the same day, because of any number of factors: tiredness, hunger, being too hot or too cold, anxiety, distracted by other activities, missing their parents, being confused about what they are being asked to do, seeing an activity as pointless or simply not wanting to comply with the adult. Such testing would seem to serve no other function that contributing towards political targets.

> When the government is forcing four year olds to endure inappropriate tests just to make it easier to rank and compare schools; and when discussions about early years focus solely on the economic benefits of getting mothers back to work, are the best interests of the child being made at a primary level?
>
> (Pre-school Learning Alliance 2015)

> The government says that it's all about school accountability but the reality is that schools start labelling children by ability at far too young an age, which will have repercussions for the rest of their schooling.
>
> (Merrick 2015)

Sarah Tomlinson at the Easter 2015 National Union of Teachers (NUT) conference asked: 'Why have so many psychologists and people in the field of mental health responded so vigorously in support of our "Too Young To Test" campaign? It is because they know the impact the tests have on children'.

> When you find the CBI [Confederation of British Industry] and the NUT on the same page as the likes of Pearson [UK exam board], all arguing that our exam dependency has got out of hand, you can be confident that you're on to something. The only people who don't seem to agree are the politicians in the Department for Education.
>
> (Mroz 2015)

There is a need to keep early testing in schools in perspective and consider the consequence of reporting such assessments on pupils to their families. When six-year-old children have school reports that refer to the child having emerging, expected levels of attainment or attainment that exceeds expectations, and yet it is known that all children develop at different rates, have different interests, strengths and weaknesses, the value of such reports must be questioned. Does the quantity of data being produced equate to an increased and comprehensive understanding of the child or merely fuel parental anxiety and promote a competitive atmosphere? When a five year old fails the Phonics Test, will the results appear on her CV? How could telling parents that their children have failed their first test at school be kind or helpful? All parents think their children are wonderful; this is nature's way of ensuring that young children thrive. When feedback from school indicates that their son or daughter may not be as wonderful as they thought, such information is certain to affect parental attitudes. Some parents will be defensive of their child and their relationships with the school become strained, even when it is acknowledged that good relationships between school and home are a vital factor in promoting pupil learning. Other parents might feel under pressure to work on additional phonics or number bonds with their child at the weekend, rather than going to the park, the swimming pool, shopping, watching TV or cooking together, playing in the garden or visiting relatives. Parents cannot be as objective about their children as teachers. Anxious parents will not make the most patient of tutors, thereby putting the parent/child relationship under unnecessary stress. Enjoying normal, everyday experiences with close family will be in the long-term interest of the child's self-esteem and happiness, but when the school pronounces judgement on their child, parents may lose confidence in their instincts. Government policies, such as fining parents for taking children out of school during term time, reinforce the idea that politicians know best and that being in the classroom is more important than spending time with the family.

When an increasing emphasis is placed on testing younger children, the implications of preparing for tests will affect the children in the previous age bracket. If we are assessing the achievements of toddlers, what are the implications in terms of preparation required by babies or pregnant women? Sir Michael Wilshaw, Ofsted's Chief Inspector said: 'What the poorest children need is to be taught, and well taught, from the age of two' (Wilshaw 2015).

All children at the age of two need love and attention from adults who are close and consistent figures in their lives, preferably family members with strong emotional attachments to the children. Many nurseries will have tick-box commitments that detract from warm, caring interaction and individually focused engagement with young children. The time spent in nurseries checking that the children are progressing would be better spent enabling the progress. Parents and families will be unaware of the targets that their children are supposed to be meeting and so can respond to their children naturally and appropriately as individuals.

\* \* \*

The five issues described above provide examples of the negative experience some pupils endure in school. When the children deal with these issues on a daily basis throughout their formative years, there will be a lasting impact on the way they perceive themselves and their worth in the eyes of others. The reality of the situation is irrelevant as it is the pupil's perception that will have the long-term effect.

Not all pupils' experience at school will be negative and many children will have a balance of pluses and minuses in terms of feedback. However, for a significant number of pupils, the minuses from school will be compounded by additional issues from their home background and social environment. This combination may prove enough to tip them into unhappiness. Solutions to the children's difficulties will need to be multifaceted. Providing counselling services for children who are unhappy because of family breakdown, examination stress, cyber bullying or body image problems puts the responsibility for the unhappiness firmly on the shoulders of the child. Input would be better directed towards those who hold responsibility for the children's stress. The need exists for increased control of social media sites, restrictions on advertising that targets children and young people, increased information for parents about child development, improved marriage guidance and relationship advice and the setting of broader educational aims for schools.

While the legislative solutions to such problems within society are the responsibility of politicians, schools have a role to play in ensuring all children grow up feeling valued and that they have a worthwhile role to play in society. If this is to happen, schools need to cater for a wider range of needs, interests and aptitudes. Schools must prepare pupils to be useful, compassionate and contented citizens, and focusing on training them to take exams and little else is shortsighted and of benefit to neither individual or society. Chapter 2 discusses perceptions of intelligence, how these perceptions have changed as society has evolved, what would be seen to constitute intelligent behaviour in the modern world and the part schools should play to promote such behaviour.

## Bibliography

Assessment Reform Group (2002) Page 4. The University of Cambridge, Faculty of Education.

Barber, L. (2015) The fifty leading business pioneers. *Financial Times*, 31 March.

Black, P. and Wiliam, D. (1998) *Inside the Black Box: Raising standards through classroom assessment.* GL Assessment.

Bond, M. (2014) The secret of success: Blood, or sweat and tears? *New Scientist*, 8 March, 221: 30–4.

Cain, S. (2012) *Quiet: The Power of Introverts in a World That Can't Stop Talking.* Danvers, MA: Crown Publishing Group.

Dabrowski, K. (1972) *Psychoneurosis Is Not an Illness.* London: Gryf.

DfE (2010) *Month of Birth and Education Schools Analysis and Research Division* Research Report. DfE-RR017.

DfE (2015) *Mental Health and Behaviour in Schools: Departmental advice for school staff.* DfE-00435-2014.

Delaney, S., Dweck, C., Chatman, J. and Kray, L. (2014) How companies can profit from a growth mindset. *Harvard Business Review*, November.

Dweck, C. (2006) *Mindset: The new psychology of success.* New York: Random House.

Geake, J. (2009) *The Brain at School.* Oxford: Oxford University Press.

Gladwell, M. (2002) The talent myth. *The New Yorker*, 22 July.

Leitch, N. (2013) Childcare ratio changes proposed by the government will make children suffer. *The Guardian*, 27 April.

Leslie, S.J., Cimpian, A., Meyer, M. and Freeland, E. (2015) Expectations of brilliance underlie gender distribution across academic disciplines. *Science*, 347(6219): 262–5.

Logan, J. (2009) Dyslexic entrepreneurs: The incidence, their coping strategies and their business skills. *Dyslexia*, 15(4): 328–46.

Merrick, B. (2015) *Experts Oppose Assessments for Four-year-olds.* BBC News, March.

Milne, D. (2000) *Teaching the Brain.* Dyslexia International e-Campus.

Mroz, A. (2015) *Times Educational Supplement Editorial*, 21 August.

Mussen, P. (1983) Piaget's theory, in P. Mussen (ed.), *Handbook of Child Psychology*, Vol. 1, 4th edition, New York: Wiley.

Nagy, Z., Westerberg, H. and Klingberg, T. (2004) Maturation of white matter is associated with the development of cognitive functions during childhood. *Cognitive Neuroscience*, 16: 1227–33.

Norbury, C., Gooch, D., Gillian, B., Charman, T., Simonoff, E. and Pickles, A. (2015) Younger children experience lower levels of language competence and academic progress in the first year of school: Evidence from a population study. *Journal of Child Psychology and Psychiatry.* doi:10.1111/jcpp.12431.

Pre-school Learning Alliance (2015) Neil Leitch Chief Executive Oficer of the PLA speaking at the Annual Pre-school Learning Alliance's annual national conference, 15 July.

RSA (2011) *Brain Waves Module 1: Neuroscience, society and policy.* London: The Royal Society.

Schools and Students Health Education Unit (2015) Young People into 2015.

Watkins, C. (2010) Learning, Performance and Improvement. Institute of Education, UK, London. Research Publication of the International Network for School Improvement. Summer 2010, issue 34, page 3.

Whitebread, D. (2012) The importance of play: A report on the value of children's play with a series of policy recommendations. Brussels: Toy Industries of Europe.

Wilshaw, M. (2015) *Early Years Annual Report.* Ofsted, July.

Wragg, T. (1998) *Times Educational Supplement*, 18 August.

Wragg, T. (2004) *Education, Education, Education: The best bits of Ted Wragg.* New York: RoutledgeFalmer.

# CHAPTER 2

# The links between attitude and intelligence

Traditional definitions of intelligence have always been related closely to success in standardised tests and examinations. It is easy to measure pupil performance against such quantitative data, but more difficult to measure performance against qualitative data such as self-efficacy, behaviour, resilience and attitude. Schools are held to account for the measureable, but a pupil's resilience and social skills, for example, may not be tested until the individual needs to cope with a difficult situation and has the opportunity to demonstrate their strength of character. Educational input does not always have immediate and obvious outcomes.

Schools are subject to political interference that often results in the setting of worthy, but misplaced, targets. Challenge and rigour are needed in education, but not always in ways that politicians appear to believe. Politicians cannot be blamed for their lack of in-depth knowledge of education and are certain to draw from their own experience of school. Those individuals who have achieved in terms of examination success will form the majority of those who rise to positions of political authority. They are likely to view educational progress and school improvement in terms of academic achievement with increased 'rigour and challenge' being required to make the exam system more stringent in order to better identify the intellectual elite. Increased opportunity for all may be seen in terms of narrow targets, such as raising the number of young people accessing higher education.

However, the overriding aim of education must be to give pupils skills for life, as opposed to a position in an outdated intellectual pecking order. When taxi drivers, solicitors, nursery nurses, gardeners, surgeons, models, priests, social workers, musicians, carpenters, authors, soldiers, actors and scientists are all members of the same class, their learning styles, personal interests and individual talents will all need to be acknowledged. Education must provide for a diversity of needs rather than focus on a specific group of pupils.

Most politicians will have been educated to degree level with Oxford University being the institution of choice within the Conservative Cabinet of 2015. Almost half of this cabinet attended Oxford (ten out of twenty-two), three Cambridge and two Bristol. The surest ticket to the top for politicians of all parties is a degree in Politics, Philosophy and Economics (PPE) from Oxford. It is inevitable that such individuals will see success in academic examinations as the route to success in life. Current Education Secretary Nicky Morgan, who read Law at St Hugh's, Oxford, said: 'We believe making GCSEs and 'A' levels more rigorous will prepare students properly for life after school.'

Unfortunately, an exam-focused education will encourage young people to become increasingly rigid in their thinking. In order to cope effectively with their workload, pupils will insist they learn only the information that is to be tested in the exam. Such a system will encourage conformity rather than creativity and innovation.

Analysis of data from PISA (Programme for International Student Assessment) rankings and the adult tests administered by OECD (Organisation for Economic Co-operation and Development) show that the average level scores achieved by UK fifteen year olds in assessments drop to significantly below average levels for sixteen to twenty-four year olds. This would suggest that the fifteen year olds have been taught to the test and their learning is purely superficial.

Pupils who are unmotivated by a constant diet of exam fodder may become disillusioned and determine never to go near anything remotely educational after leaving school, reducing the likelihood of lifelong learning.

Success in exams does not guarantee career satisfaction or personal happiness and so cannot be the only aim of education. Statistics on graduate performance show that in 2004, 40 per cent of graduates were in non-graduate jobs and by 2010 almost 60 per cent of graduates were in non-graduate jobs.

(CIPD 2015)

A university degree cannot ensure employment security, remove stress from an individual's life or add to their well-being. Businesses and local councils may stand to benefit more from the expansion of Higher Education than the young people directly involved. Many factors are at play and the consideration of young people and their future will not always be a priority. Private investors will be happy to develop the facilities of new universities, converting redundant office blocks into hostels or building high-density student accommodation in rundown areas of cities. The advantages of such expansion will include: the creation of new jobs in areas that may be suffering from high unemployment, student cash invigorating the local economy, and the regeneration of areas of cities that may have been shunned by local residents. Private investors will receive secure and generous returns through student rents or by selling individual units to smaller investors.

When so many different groups have an interest in developing university education for all, the need exists for comprehensive and unbiased careers advice to ensure young people are informed of the complete range of qualifications and career paths open to them. Unfortunately, funding for careers education has been radically reduced in schools nationwide. A UNISON survey in June 2014 revealed that 83 per cent of the schools surveyed no longer employed a careers adviser. Without careers advice, young people will continue to apply to university out of fear that their employment prospects will be limited if they do not have a degree. Employers will continue to use degrees as part of their initial recruitment process to screen for positions that previously would have required GCSEs or 'A' Levels. The anxieties of today's university students will reflect those of previous generations of undergraduates: relationships, home sickness and the practical problems of cooking and cleaning, in addition to new concerns relating to future employment and the expense of daily living. The student loan system has meant that most students incur a high level of debt, with many leaving university with a £40,000+ loan to repay. Even when the young person takes a poorly paid job and fails to reach the threshold for repayment of the loan, the debt will be accruing interest. This is a depressing start to adult life, putting extra pressure on students in terms of validating their university experience.

Everyone, no matter their academic or social background, is certain to have to cope with upsetting circumstances during their lives: death within their immediate family, redundancy, illness, divorce or life-changing accidents. Making academic achievement the only aspirational goal for pupils in schools is inappropriate and short-sighted. Everyone, including those graduates heading for professions in banking, medicine, politics, law and business, will need additional qualities: empathy, resilience, problem-solving ability, creativity, listening skills and an understanding of what constitutes moral behaviour. Opportunities to develop such characteristics need to be embedded in everyday classroom provision.

Research from the CBI shows that 60 per cent of employers are dissatisfied with school leavers' self-management skills (CBI 2014). A report by the CBI in 2007 placed value on employees possessing qualities such as emotional intelligence, optimism and determination.

The original view of intelligence was based on IQ (intelligence quotient) testing. IQ refers to the score achieved by an individual when completing certain standardised tests. A French psychologist called Alfred Binet invented the first intelligence test, the Binet-Simon scale, early in the twentieth century.

Lewis Terman, an American psychologist, believed that IQ was inherited and was the strongest predictor of an individual's ultimate success in life. Terman started a longitudinal study on 1,500 children who had achieved a high score in IQ tests in Californian schools in the 1920s. The results revealed little about the long-term implications of possessing a high IQ, with the exception of one study by Terman's

associate, Melita Oden. In 1968, Oden compared the 100 most successful and the 100 least successful individuals in the group, defining
success as holding jobs that required their intellectual gifts. The successful and non-successful groups did not differ in terms of IQ, but
did in levels of confidence, persistence and parental encouragement.
However, even Terman had reservations about the misuse of IQ assessment and warned against a total reliance on tests.

An individual's strength of character is as important as their IQ score
in terms of their academic achievement. Duckworth and Seligman
(2002) conducted research with a group of American thirteen year olds
into the effect of IQ and self-discipline on the pupils' school grades.
The conclusion of the research was that self-discipline explained twice
as much of the variation in pupil grades as levels of IQ.

Paul Torrance (1980), an American psychologist, followed the
lives of several hundred individuals who had been identified as high
achievers, from secondary school into middle age during the second
half of the twentieth century. Torrance discovered that it was not the
individual's academic ability that led to success in adult life, but their
thinking skills, creativity, ability to work independently and having
an intense interest in one specific field.

During the second half of the twentieth century, theories of intelligence became more complex and the need for the individual to possess
additional attitudes increasingly apparent.

By the 1980s Gardner was recommending adopting a broader, more
inclusive view of intelligence, acknowledging the importance of several different types of intelligence: musical, visual–spatial, verbal
linguistic, logical mathematical, kinaesthetic, interpersonal, intraper-
sonal, naturalistic, existential and moral. In Robert Sternberg's triarchic
theory of intelligence (1985), he describes three types of intelligence
that he believed needed to combine to create success in life.

- Analytical intelligence. Traditional IQ tests would measure this
  type of thinking.
- Experiential/creative intelligence. Creative, divergent thinking,
  the ability to generate new ideas and deal with novel situations.

- Contextual/practical intelligence. The ability to apply intelligence and knowledge to problem-solving tasks in the real world.

Renzulli's (1978) three ringed conception of giftedness shows what he believes are the three traits necessary for intelligent behaviour: an above-average ability, creativity and task commitment. If high achievement is to occur, these three skills will need to work in partnership.

1   Above-average abilities. It is only necessary to be clever enough. Renzulli does not completely reject tests of general intellectual ability, but says that IQ test results need to be kept in perspective.
2   Creativity. An individual's degree of flexibility, originality of thought, openness to experience and willingness to take risks.
3   Task commitment. The individual's ability to persevere, work hard and their level of interest in a subject. In his book *Outliers* (2008), Malcolm Gladwell makes reference to the '10,000 Hour Rule', claiming that the key to mastery in any particular field is a matter of practising and honing skills for a total of at least 10,000 hours.

Nothing in this world can take the place of persistence. Talent will not; nothing is more common than unsuccessful people with talent. Genius will not; unrewarded genius is almost a proverb. Education will not; the world is full of educated derelicts.

(Calvin Coolidge, American President, 1923–1929)

## Habits of Mind

Numerous lists of the different attitudes and attributes believed necessary for a full and successful life have been set out by psychologists and educationalists. The sixteen Habits of Mind identified by Costa and Kellick (2000) refer to those skills that help an individual cope successfully with novel situations or know how to behave when an answer is not obvious. The habits include:

- Being able to think about thinking.
- Being persistent.

- Managing impulsivity.
- Listening with understanding and empathy.
- Creating, imagining, innovating.
- Thinking flexibly.
- Questioning and posing problems.
- Remaining open to continuous learning.
- Being motivated.

## What is mindset?

According to Claxton (2002), 'Intelligence is as much a matter of determination and self discipline as of intellect'. Claxton's *'Building Learning Power'* introduces four 'Rs':

1   Resilience. Coping with difficulty and frustration.
2   Resourcefulness. Having a variety of learning strategies to hand and knowing when to use them.
3   Reflection. Understanding one's learning strategies and thinking about how they might be improved.
4   Reciprocity. Working in collaboration, listening to others and having empathy with their point of view.

## Positive psychology

Positive psychology is a branch of psychology that developed rapidly towards the end of the twentieth century. Positive psychology focuses on the development of a satisfactory life rather than on the treatment of anxiety and depression. Anders Ericsson and Martin Seligman are two major exponents of this approach. Ericsson argues that having an IQ level of over 120 does not equate to a higher level of happiness, as an individual only needs to be clever enough. Seligman proposes that kindness, gratitude and a capacity for affection are more closely linked to well-being than intelligence or educational achievement.

Such definitions of intelligent behaviour and personal contentment have implications for schools, what they should teach and how this should be taught. Current theories of intelligence group the attitudes and attributes of an intelligent person under the following broad headings:

1   Metacognition or being able to think about thinking. When pupils use metacognition in school they will examine the ways in which they plan, monitor and assess their performance. Thinking about thinking enables pupils to adapt and improve, helping them to realise that they have control over their learning.
2   Possessing good social skills. Having the ability to work collaboratively, to listen to and have empathy with others. Research points to the importance of the role played by parents in establishing such skills.
3   Being self-confident. In order to develop self-discipline, pupils must have an adequate level of self-confidence. This will be built on an understanding of their own personality: how they can control their emotions, delay gratification, motivate themselves, develop persistence, and deal with failure and disappointment.
4   Being creative. Having curiosity, being able to generate new ideas, knowing how to deal with novel situations, being flexible, having originality of thought. The ability to apply intelligence and knowledge in the real world.

The discussion above would point to an individual's attitude and self-efficacy being more important for a successful, fulfilled life than a high IQ score. An acceptance of broad definitions of intelligence has implications for the curriculum. The hidden curriculum, those values and beliefs conveyed almost inadvertently through the classroom context, will need to be afforded the same level of importance as the content of the subject curriculum. Section II discusses how the areas of metacognition, social skills, self-confidence and creativity could be promoted in mainstream schools and integrated into classroom provision.

# Bibliography

CBI (2014) *Gateway to Growth.* CBI/Pearson Education and Skills Survey.

Claxton, G. (2002) *Building Learning Power: Helping young people become better learners.* Bristol: TLO.

Colvin, G. (2008) *Talent is Overrated: What really separates world-class performers from everybody else.* London: Nicholas Brealey Publishing.

Costa, A. (1991) *The Search for Intelligent Life.* Alexandria, VA: Association for Supervision and Curriculum Development.

Costa A.L. and Kallick, B. (2000) *Habits of Mind: A developmental series.* Victoria, Australia: Hawker Brownlow Education Pty Ltd.

CIPD. (2015) *Over-qualification and Skills Mismatch in the Graduate Labour Market.* London: CIPD.

Duckworth, A. and Seligman, M. (2002) *Self-discipline Outdoes IQ in Predicting Academic Performance of Adolescents.* Philadelphia: Positive Psychology Centre, University of Pennsylvania.

Dweck, C.S. (2006) *Mindset: The new psychology of success.* New York: Random House.

Gardner, H. (1993) *Multiple Intelligences: The theory in practice.* New York: Basic Books.

Gardner, H. (1983) *Frames of Mind.* New York: Basic Books.

Gladwell, M. (2008) *Outliers.* Boston, MA: Little, Brown and Company.

Renzulli, J.S. (1978) What Makes Giftedness? Re-examining a definition. *Phi Delta Kappan*, 60 (3): 180–184, 261.

Sternberg, R. (1985) *Beyond IQ: A triarchic theory of human intelligence.* New York: Cambridge University Press.

Torrance, E.P. (1980) Growing up creatively gifted: The 22-year longitudinal study. *The Creative Child and Adult Quarterly*, 3: 148–58.

# Developing pupils' self-confidence and emotional well-being within the mainstream context

Theories of intelligence group the attitudes and attributes of an intelligent individual under four broad headings: metacognition, social skills, self-confidence and creativity. Enabling pupils to cultivate these skills in schools will help them academically, socially and emotionally. When the importance of the *process* of learning and the *process* of teaching are recognised, the importance of the 'hidden curriculum' of schools becomes increasingly apparent.

# CHAPTER 3

# Metacognition

Metacognition relates to an individual's ability to monitor their own learning. John Flavell, an American psychologist, first used the term metacognition in 1979 to describe the process of thinking about thinking. When pupils use metacognitive strategies, they will examine the ways in which they plan, monitor and assess their performance. Thinking about their thinking will enable pupils to adapt and improve their learning, helping them to realise that they have control over their performance in school and beyond.

## Key point

It is important that discussion of metacognitive strategies occurs in the mainstream classroom to ensure that pupils perceive learning about how to learn to be of equal importance to the acquisition of subject knowledge.

## Stand-alone thinking programmes

An increase in research into thinking skills and metacognition in the second half of the twentieth century led to the development of numerous stand-alone programmes designed specifically to support pupils' thinking in schools.

### Instrumental Enrichment – Feuerstein

Feuerstein (1999) was a clinical psychologist, best known for his work with young victims of the Holocaust in Israel after the Second World

War. Feuerstein believed that intelligence was not fixed and could be modified. His 'Instrumental Enrichment' programme is based on the principle that thinking skills can be taught directly. Instrumental Enrichment aims to assist the development of thinking processes through supporting the learner in the understanding of different types of thinking, increasing their intrinsic motivation and helping them to develop reflective approaches to their learning, changing pupils from passive to active learners.

## CoRT (Cognitive Research Trust) programme – de Bono

Edward de Bono (1985) is a psychologist who has devised numerous thinking skills programmes, one example of which would be his Six Thinking Hats. This is a problem-solving approach in which pupils are taught to look at problems using hats to symbolise different types of thinking. Six different lines of enquiry symbolised by hats are identified and each assigned a colour. When the pupil wears that colour of 'hat', they look at the problem from a specific angle:

1   When wearing the *white* hat, pupils ask questions and consider all the information available.
2   The *red* hat is used for an emotional approach, with pupils following instinctive 'gut' reactions or feelings.
3   The *black* hat is used to judge any negative points, and for the identification of flaws or barriers.
4   *Yellow* is used to examine positives and identify benefits.
5   The *green* hat is for thinking about the problem creatively using lateral thinking.
6   The *blue* hat symbolises the final approach or overview: 'Have we looked at the problem from all possible angles?'

Other approaches to thinking from the CoRT programme would include PMI and CAF. PMI considers the Pluses, Minuses and Interesting factors, while the CAF approach reminds pupils of the importance of 'Consider All Factors'.

## CASE (Cognitive Acceleration through Science Education)

The CASE project was devised in the 1980s by academics at King's College School of Education as an intervention strategy, and combined teaching curriculum topics with cognitive acceleration methods. Pupils were helped to move through Piagetian stages from a concrete stage of thinking to the formal processing of information. They were encouraged to reflect on their own thinking processes and apply this thinking to other contexts. The focus of the programme being how pupils learn, rather than what they learn.

## Philosophy for Children

This programme devised by Matthew Lipman (1976) involves reading philosophical stories to children to encourage deeper thinking through discussion about the texts as facilitated by the teacher.

## UK Resilience Programme Project (2007–2010)

Trials of the programme began in 2007 and, although evaluation of the project in 2010 showed numerous positive short-term results, no long-term beneficial effects for participants were recorded.

\*\*\*

In recent years, there has been a shift of emphasis towards an inclusive and integrated approach to the teaching of thinking skills with the realisation that, if all pupils are to be given the opportunity to develop metacognition, opportunities for development and practice must be embedded in the mainstream curriculum. Stand-alone programmes will only reach those pupils who are involved in the programmes and are only as good as the teacher delivering them. When metacognition is promoted across all subjects, pupils will be more inclined to incorporate it into their everyday learning.

To use metacognitive strategies in the mainstream classroom, pupils will need to have an understanding of their personal strengths and weaknesses and possess a reasonable grasp of generic study skills. Teaching staff will need to provide effective feedback to enable pupils to improve their performance and use questioning to extend pupils' thinking skills.

Pupils will need to be aware of themselves as learners and of their personal learning strengths and weaknesses. Without such understanding, they may believe that their learning capacity is fixed and that 'cleverness' or 'stupidity' is a permanent state. If they believe their intelligence is fixed, they will not feel a need to reflect upon their learning.

Discussion of the differences between personal learning preferences will help pupils to realise that all learners are individuals and that they should focus on improving their own performance rather than comparing themselves to others. Pupils will learn from discussion with peers about individual strengths and weaknesses. For example:

- Are they good in discussions but find it hard to get their ideas down on paper? Why might that be? What could they do to help themselves?
- Can they understand concepts when taught in a practical way, but lose concentration when the lesson is chalk and talk? Why might that be? What can they do to help themselves? How do other pupils deal with this problem?
- What motivates them to learn and what do they find demotivating? Why might that be? What can they do to help themselves?
- Do they work best in short bursts with regular breaks or can they sustain concentration for longer periods? Why might that be? What can they do to help themselves?
- Can they concentrate with music playing in the background or do they need silence to focus? Why might that be and does it matter?
- Do they prefer regular short assessments or one exam at the end of the year? Why might that be and does it matter?
- Do they have any weaknesses in essay planning, revision, concentration, presentation, reading speed, handwriting, comprehension or note-taking? How severe is their need? Is their difficulty a constant concern or can their anxiety be temporary? Are their weaknesses common to all subjects or just a few? Why might that be? What can they do to help themselves?

Such discussions will increase a teacher's understanding of a pupil's learning styles and give important feedback about the appropriateness of their teaching style. Could their approach be adapted to better meet the needs of different groups of learners? What strengths do pupils possess that they could use to help themselves or offer as an aid to peers?

- An artistic ability that enables them to create attractive revision materials.
- An understanding of IT that helps with personal organisation.
- Social skills that enable them to work collaboratively.
- Hobbies outside of school that enable them to relax and unwind.
- A burning ambition or personal target they could use for motivation.
- The ability to work hard.

It is important that pupils understand the basic principles of how the brain works. This can be discussed in lessons as related to a specific aspect of learning, for example, memory and revision techniques. Every time the class has information to learn for a test or assessment, use a five-minute plenary to remind pupils of how to revise. Points to raise might include:

- The brain will notice and remember the unusual, rather than the ordinary. Transform linear notes into highlighted bullet points, summaries on file cards, mind maps or question/answer cards.
- In order to make sense of information, the brain needs to connect new knowledge with what is already known. Link new information to old knowledge to secure overall understanding of the topic: what you have learnt about this subject in previous years or have observed in everyday situations.
- Recall is strengthened when information is regularly revisited. Revision is most effective when carried out through a little but often approach. Twenty minutes each evening for a week will be a more effective way to learn and retain knowledge than cramming for an hour at the last minute.
- It is difficult to learn effectively when you are distracted, tired, uncomfortable or hungry. Try to reduce distractions before you

start work. If a worrying thought comes into your head, note it down on a piece of paper to come back later and get back to the task in hand.

- All revision methods work best when they are *active*; that is when the brain has to think about the facts and do something with the information, perhaps creating diagrams, comic strips or timelines, rather than just reading information through. For active learning activities to use in mainstream lessons, see Section IV, 'Active learning techniques'.
- For discussion points relating to the brain, see Section IV, 'The brain and learning'.

Pupils need to possess the study skills required to be independent learners and to know how to improve and adapt their performance as necessary. Facts and knowledge are part of education, but many pupils will need help to acquire the separate set of skills necessary to record, memorise, understand, manipulate and reproduce information and to identify those areas in which they need help. It is important that teachers take an enabling role rather than provide answers to encourage pupils to take responsibility for their learning; for example, many pupils will not do reading homework because their reading is too slow and they know that the task will take an inordinate amount of time. Open discussion about such difficulty in class will help pupils to see they are not alone, and raise awareness among staff of the common problems experienced by the children of which they may be unaware.

If the pupil feels their reading speed is comparatively slow:

- Do they know anyone else with the same problem and how do they cope with their difficulty?
- Is there advice available on the internet?
- Are there books on reading speed in the school library?
- Has the pupil always had this problem or has it developed as their work load has increased?
- How do their parents or siblings manage if they have to read a lot of text quickly?
- See what suggestions other members of the class can make.

Encourage pupils to discuss and think about what works best for them, in what situation and for what subjects. Such discussion will encourage a pupil's confidence in their own ability by showing their opinion to be valid and valued. Discussion does not have to be whole class, but can be in pairs or small groups. All pupil talk will increase pupil engagement in lessons and raise awareness of the commonality of difficulties. General discussion about coping strategies used by their peers may provide advice the pupils had not previously considered:

> I find it useful to jot down a brief overview at the end of every History lesson summarising in my own words what we've covered. Then I file those summaries at the end of my class notes to help me remember what we talked about when I need to revise.
>
> I borrow CDs or DVDs of English set texts from the school library. I have found that if I listen to or watch them it helps me to understand what is happening and who the different characters are.
>
> I know I tend to just read the words and can miss underlying messages in books. If I can watch a DVD, I can get a better idea of what is being suggested, but not actually said.
>
> In French, I try to learn ten new words every week. I don't worry about any unusual words because I know that would be too much for me, but learning ten words that come up all the time helps me to keep on top of things.
>
> I really don't understand a lot of topics in Physics, so I ask my older brother to explain it to me in a simpler way. He draws pictures to help explain and I keep those in my file.
>
> When I'm revising Geography, I go through my notes, highlight important points in red, any subject vocabulary I should know in green and draw boxes around any statistics. Anything to make it look less boring!

Teaching pupils that working with others and asking friends, family or adults for help is a sensible approach to take and does not constitute cheating, but rather intelligent behaviour. Teaching staff can demonstrate their own willingness to refer to others by involving specialist staff in their lessons. Perhaps the librarian can teach independent research skills and how to use alternative materials, such as directories, catalogues, bibliographies, anthologies and encyclopaedias, or access external sources of information, such as government agencies or church and museum records.

Scaffolding or demonstrating by the teacher or another pupil is a useful way of showing pupils how to tackle unfamiliar tasks. There is no point in telling a child to revise more thoroughly, to learn their French vocabulary, to think about their spelling or to include evidence in essays, when they have little idea of how to do this. For example, young children may need to be shown how to make their writing neater by tackling their presentation in a step-by-step way. First, sit your writing on the line. Then make the spaces between the words bigger. Then make the writing itself slightly larger. Then look at the ascenders and make them taller. Older pupils could be given practical advice about personal organisation (see Section IV, 'Organisation: how to help pupils to organise themselves'.

In secondary school, teachers may have read hundreds of GCSE essays and so the required structure will seem obvious to them, but it may be the first time a pupil has tackled this level of essay and they have little idea about the appropriate format. It is wise initially to scaffold approaches for pupils to take: how to structure an English essay, how to write up a science experiment, or how to research and record information for coursework. The pupils can file such guidelines to refer to in the future. Some of the approaches will be specific to subjects, for example, how to plan an English Literature 'A' Level essay, and others will be generically useful, for example, how to take notes from a textbook.

Other pupils can be a useful source of support; they will be at the same stage or just beyond that of their peers and are likely to understand why they are experiencing a problem and be able to explain solutions in everyday, rather than specialist, language.

## Scaffolding note-taking

The class talks through various note-taking methods then collates their ideas on a prompt sheet for future reference. The following example is a Learning Support Department prompt sheet:

1  When taking notes from a book, always look at the publication date to check the information is current. This is particularly relevant in … Chemistry/IT … where information is continually updated.

2  Always record the page number because it makes it easier to check back later. Noting down page numbers is a good habit to get into and will be useful in the future.

3  Try using blank postcards as bookmarks and jot down facts on cards while reading. When the card is full, start a new one.

4  Keep these postcard notes together with a treasury tag. Read the cards aloud, highlighting any key information when revising. Reading the cards aloud will force you to slow down and read more carefully, and you will be hearing the information as well as seeing it and saying it.

5  Write out a summary of notes or draw a mind map on one side of A4 to show how all the information fits together. Keep these sheets with the original notes.

6  When taking notes from a borrowed textbook, photocopy the important pages and highlight any relevant information on the paper copy.

7  If you can't write quickly enough to take notes in class, concentrate on listening and photocopy a friend's notes after the lesson.

8  Skim read texts before starting to make notes. The text may not contain any relevant information.

9  Read to the end of a passage and then write the information down in your own words. This will make your notes easier to understand at a later date.

10  Keep notes in a file in sequential order. Filing work neatly saves time in the long run.

## Scaffolding for comprehension

The class talks through any methods they have found helpful then collates their ideas on a prompt sheet for future reference. The following is an example of Pupil A's prompt sheet:

1 When I don't understand written information in books, I see if I can find any pictures or diagrams to help me. Diagrams can show how facts are linked and may be easier to understand than pages of writing.

2 I try to put the information into my own words. I stop at the end of each section and ask myself what it was about. If I can't talk about what I've read, I know I haven't really understood it.

3 I often ask my friends to explain things to me; sometimes they can put difficult ideas into everyday words.

4 I read any really difficult passages aloud very slowly, sometimes sentence by sentence.

5 If there is an easier book that covers the same topic, I read that first. I used to read my little brother's Key Stage 2 Science book when I was doing Key Stage 3 Biology.

6 Sometimes chapters will have summaries or conclusions, maybe in the first or last paragraph. I read those first to try to get an overview.

7 If I don't know what a word means and I can't guess from the passage, I look it up. Often text books have a glossary of words at the back of the book.

8 I try to learn the meanings of words that are used a lot in subjects. The more words I understand, the better my comprehension of that subject becomes.

9 If the book is fiction and there are a lot of characters with confusing names, I make a list of the characters, sketch a picture of what I think they look like or jot down a description of them and the part they play in the story. I keep that sheet next to the book as I read.

10 I see if the library has any DVDs of the set English texts and watch those to get an idea of what happens in the book. Sometimes the library may have CDs of the story or be able to stream texts for pupils.

## Scaffolding for reading speed

The class talks through how they help themselves to read quickly then collates their ideas on a prompt sheet for future reference. The following is an example of Pupil J's prompt sheet:

1 I look for headings and key words first to get the overall sense of the passage.
2 I look at the titles of chapters, skim over summaries and conclusions and don't bother reading anything that isn't relevant.
3 I look out for any pictures or diagrams that will explain sections of the text.
4 I try to read blocks of three or four words at a time.
5 I track the sentences steadily across the page with a ruler, piece of paper or my finger and keep my eyes moving at that pace. I try not to go back and re-read.
6 I remove distractions, shut the door, switch off my phone and turn off any music and make myself focus.
7 I tell myself that I will really concentrate on reading, but only for ten minutes, and then have a break.
8 I make sure the room is light enough. My eyes get tired quickly if the light is dim.
9 I sometimes chew a sweet as I read because that stops me from pronouncing every word in my head.
10 I try to learn the meanings of common subject words. When I come across them in texts and don't know what they mean, it slows my reading down.

## Scaffolding methods of learning spellings

The class talks through useful ways of remembering spellings then collates the ideas on a prompt sheet for future reference. The following is an example from Form 5 JE's prompt sheet:

1 Use the 'Look, cover, write and check' method we used in Year 2. Look at the word, cover it over, write it out and then check you've spelt it correctly. Repeat the process several times.

2 Make up mnemonics. You can't separate a para from his chute. The secretary knows a secret. The accommodation has two cots and two mattresses (two cs and two ms).

3 Think of other words that look or sound similar: knight, fright, slight, alright, midnight.

4 Pronounce the word in a different way, for example, E – G – Y – P – T spells Egypt. Choc-O-late.

5 Draw a picture of the spelling with the letters as part of the picture. Current or currant? Which is the word associated with electricity? Write out the word 'currEnt' with electric wires running parallel to the crossbars in the capital E.

6 Divide the word into syllables and say the different parts aloud as you write them down. It doesn't matter how you separate the sounds in the word as long as it makes sense to you. Re – pre – sent or rep – res – ent spells 'represent'.

7 Write the spelling out over and over again, saying the letter names aloud as you write.

8 Shut your eyes and imagine the word written in colour on the wall. See if you can spell the word backwards to check that you really have a good mental picture of the sequence of letters in the spelling.

9 Look for words or groups of letters within the word: fat/her, Carib/bean, Medi/terra/nean, to/get/her, environ/ment.

10 Trace over the word several times with coloured pens or pencils to get the feel of its shape. Look carefully at the word and decide which colour makes the spelling clearest.

## Scaffolding revision

Have a class discussion about revision methods, explaining that we all learn in different ways. Pupils may use different methods to their friends, teachers or family members and they should feel free to experiment with alternative approaches. Their preference for revision method may change for different subjects. The following is an example from Form 11 AE's prompt sheet:

1 Older pupils in senior school are able to concentrate for 30–40 minutes. There is no point trying to revise when you are not focused, so build regular breaks and variety into revision sessions. Take a 'little but often' approach to learning.

2 It is easier to revise when files are well ordered. Taking time to sort and put files into order is a valid way to start revision as you will be thinking about how different topics fit together.

3 Make up mnemonics, draw mind maps or create summaries as end-of-topic overviews. Doing something with the information will make the facts more memorable rather than simply reading notes through.

4 Mix sessions revising easy topics with sessions spent revising ones you find more difficult.

5 Make information as visually appealing as possible: bullet points, numbering, different writing or font styles, drawings, lists, or use different coloured pens and highlighters. Computer programs can produce appealing notes, but don't allow yourself to be distracted from your task.

6 Make revision cards. Ask friends or family to test you on the cards. Read them aloud, turn them over and rewrite the cards to test yourself, recite the information from memory or make new cards from the old ones.

7 It is always worth making a real effort to get to grips with understanding information. The more you understand, the less you will have to learn by rote. Take time to think about topics and how they link together or how they can be used in the real world. Thinking around information is a valid way to revise.

8 Look at old papers to see the sort of questions that examiners ask and practise answering them in the time allowed. This may seem boring, but will give you a good insight into how exam questions are worded.

9 Revise with others while you go shopping, for a walk or a bike ride. You do not have to sit indoors to learn. Discussing the topics with friends will help to consolidate your thinking: what should

be done about coastal erosion, the Arab–Israeli conflict or global warming?

10 Use IT. Online revision programs and apps add variety to revision and, although they tend not to be detailed, they will be interactive and likely to hold your attention.

## Scaffolding concentration

Have a class discussion about concentration. Different pupils will have different levels of concentration, but everyone is capable of concentrating on things they find interesting. How long is it possible to concentrate on a computer game or an interesting phone call? It is up to the pupil to learn ways to help themselves focus when they are not particularly engaged by a topic. To help pupils with their listening skills in mainstream lessons, see Section IV, 'Developing pupils' listening and attention skills'. The following is an example of Form 8 HB's prompt sheet:

1 It is your responsibility to pay attention, so make an effort to concentrate. You will not remember what has been said in a lesson if you are talking to friends.

2 When other pupils distract you, try not to sit near them. Some people find it easier to sit at the front of the class with their back to friends. Others prefer to sit at the back of the class where it is possible to see everything that is going on, rather than speculate about what interesting things might be happening behind you.

3 Ask if you can open a window to keep the room well ventilated. You are more likely to stay alert if there is a good supply of fresh air.

4 Make yourself participate in lessons: think of questions to ask or give your point of view in discussions. If you do not understand, ask. There will be other pupils who do not understand and if no one asks for clarification, the teacher will continue to teach in the same way, perhaps not realising their approach needs to change.

5 When you are not asked a question directly, think how you would have answered questions set to other pupils.

6  Be determined to concentrate. Teachers are only human and if they can see that you are making an effort, they will be more inclined to help you.

7  When working at home, make sure you have everything you need before you start to minimise distractions. Turn off your mobile, have a supply of pens and pencils available, open the window, have a drink and snack to hand and shut the door.

8  If you suddenly remember something else you have to do, do not allow yourself to go off-task, make a note of the interrupting thought and then refocus on the task in hand.

9  If your mind is wandering, saying aloud to yourself 'Stop. You must think carefully about this' may be enough to refocus your attention.

10  Make activities short and concentrated. Use a stopwatch to time yourself. It is easier to focus when you know that the time you are spending on an activity is limited. I'll make really good notes on this for fifteen minutes and then I'll get something to eat.

## Scaffolding test-taking techniques

Run through the ways to approach tests or exams until the pupil uses techniques automatically. Many pupils panic in test situations and the more automatic their responses, the more confident they will feel. The following is an example of a History Department's prompt sheet:

1  Take time to read the paper thoroughly and check the instructions carefully.

2  Look to see if the questions have a mark value and ensure you spend the appropriate amount of time on each question.

3  Plan your use of time. Put your watch on the table in front of you where it is clearly visible.

4  Decide which questions look possible and which look more complicated, then start with the easier ones.

5  If your mind goes blank, jot down a few names, dates and keywords to kick start your memory.

6 Sketch a rough plan or make a few bullet points for any longer answers before you start to write. This will save time in the long run as your work will be less rambling and more focussed.

7 Underline the keywords in questions such as describe, contrast, summarise, list or compare. Then concentrate on answering the question that has been set rather than one you would have liked. Refer back to the question a few times to make sure you are not going off at a tangent.

8 Use diagrams if appropriate, as they may explain your ideas more clearly than words.

9 Do not waste time worrying about how much anyone else is writing, concentrate on your own answers.

10 Do not ruminate on what went wrong in the last exam; that is not within your power to change. Focus on the next exam where your effort can make a difference.

*** 

It is essential that appropriate feedback is given to pupils. John Hattie (2008) carried out a comprehensive survey of the results of over 50,000 research studies into influences on pupils' learning, and concluded that the most powerful single influence affecting pupil achievement is good quality feedback. Feedback is essential if pupils are to learn from their mistakes and improve their performance. Feedback can be delivered through *summative* assessments when the pupil's performance is graded against other pupils and a pre-set benchmark, for example, the pupil gets a mark of 65 per cent, 13/20, or through *formative* assessment when the pupil's performance is used to modify future teaching to match pupil need, such as: 'This essay is much better. You have made all of the main points as we discussed in class. Now you need to add examples to show how each point can be applied.'

Both types of feedback have a role to play in the classroom, but feedback from summative assessment tends to motivate only those who anticipate success. Pupils will look at their grade, 9/10, 11/20, 54 per cent, and then compare their mark to their friends' results.

They are less likely to read teachers' comments and will continue to make the same errors.

Improvements in summative assessment are often attributed to teaching staff teaching to the test rather than to any improvement in pupils' learning. In terms of pupil metacognition, formative assessment is considered to be the more useful approach, with assessment focussed on how to progress learning rather than looking at where the learner is in relation to their peers. All assessment should help the pupil develop their skills and will need to:

- be valid, fair and consistent
- encourage dialogue between pupils, their peer group and their teachers
- measure understanding and application rather than technique and memory
- be conducted throughout the course rather than at the end
- be aimed at developing key skills
- be practical and manageable for staff and pupils.

Formative assessment could include such activities as: pre- and post-topic quizzes, observation of the way in which pupils learn and transfer their learning, pupil questionnaires and evaluation sheets, video recordings, online feedback, pupil interviews, extension projects, comparison of work with that of previous cohorts, or pupil diaries and log books. An increase in formative assessment would mean more:

- variety of assessment tools
- opportunities for pupils to take responsibility for their own learning
- clarification of learning goals and advice as to what the pupil's next steps should be
- encouragement for pupils to judge their work by how much they have learnt and the progress they have made
- assessment that is relevant to the pupils' level of ability, understanding and the work that has been covered
- appreciation of pupil effort

- support for pupils to understand assessment criteria and judge their own work through the use of self- and peer-assessment
- collaboration.

An increase in formative assessment would mean less:

- definition of the curriculum in terms of test content
- emphasis on marks and judgement of work in terms of grades
- pupil anxiety impairing test performance
- emphasis of competition for marks and grades among pupils
- emphasis on the quantity and presentation of work over pupils' learning
- emphasis on marks over advice.

Feedback should incorporate comments about the way a pupil has tackled the work or shown a positive attitude. 'I appreciate that you find learning Spanish vocabulary difficult; you must have put in a lot of effort to remember so much.' 'I realise that presenting in front of the class isn't your favourite activity, but your talk really was excellent.'

Questioning is one useful way to gauge pupils' levels of understanding. Research by Wragg and Brown (2001) found that teachers ask up to 400 questions each day amounting to approximately 70,000 questions in a year. However, between 30 per cent and 60 per cent of these questions were procedural and used to keep the lesson moving. 'Who has finished?' 'How much longer have we got?' 'Is that your book?' Reviews by Cotton (1988) of research projects on questioning in the classroom found that, when the proportion of higher order questioning was increased to 50 per cent, significant gains were made in terms of pupils' attitudes and performance.

Through good-quality questioning, the teacher will be able to collect evidence about the pupils' overall comprehension and what they do, do not or partially understand. Activities such as brainstorming, open-ended tasks, quizzes and pre-module challenges can be used to determine prior understanding before starting new topics. This will help to ensure that pupils are progressing at a rate appropriate for their level of ability and understanding. They will not have to work at a level where the information will make no sense to them or be marking time repeating work they have already covered.

The use of open-ended questions will require pupils to apply ideas and give reasons for their answers. Active involvement and participation should be expected from pupils and questions encouraged. Teachers will need to know what pupils understand, rather than what they can recall and so activities will need to be challenging enough to make the pupil think, perhaps applying the ideas they have to a new context or from a different viewpoint, such as: 'What is the same and what is different about tourism in Scotland, Spain and Switzerland?' 'What would the environmental consequences be for the local area of extending Heathrow airport rather than Gatwick airport?'

Quality questioning requires more than the simple recall of information: 'Is it always true that it is sunny when there is high pressure?', rather than 'What weather is associated with high pressure?' Good questioning will require the pupil to think about the information and then to apply their knowledge. Questions need to be designed to promote follow-up discussion: 'But what if ...?', 'Why do you think that?' or 'Will that always be the case?'

Educational psychologist, Benjamin Bloom (1956) devised a hierarchy of questioning, with recall of knowledge seen as the least demanding form of questioning and the evaluation of information as the most challenging. The hierarchy is known as Bloom's Taxonomy.

1  Knowledge question words would include list, state, identify, name and recognise. 'Identify the noun in this sentence.'
2  Comprehension question words would include summarise, explain, interpret, describe and put into your own words. 'Explain what happened to the salt when we added the water.'
3  Examples of application questioning words include classify, solve, illustrate, relate and apply. 'How could we use this fact to solve this new problem?'
4  Examples of analysis questioning words include compare, contrast, distinguish, analyse and organise. 'Why is that café more successful than this café?'

5 Examples of synthesis questioning words include design, report, discuss, create and devise. 'How well does this piece of music create a sense of happiness?'

6 Examples of evaluation questioning words include evaluate, estimate, judge, criticise and justify. 'Is there a better solution to this problem? How could you justify your answer?'

There are many simple ways in which questions can be reframed to ensure pupils are not simply regurgitating facts with little or no understanding. Higher order questions can be structured to suit the level, age and experience of the individual. To ensure everyone is participating, pupils could discuss their thoughts in pairs or small groups before answering.

1 Right and wrong.
   1 Why does this serve go over the net and this one does not?
   2 Why are these shapes quadrilaterals and these not?
   3 Why is Meal A healthier than Meal B?
   4 Why is a dandelion a weed but a daffodil is not?
   5 Why is this calculation right and this one wrong?

2 Range of answers.
   1 Are all of these foodstuffs good for you? Chocolate, potatoes, milk, bacon, sugar, salt, vegetable oil, bananas, rice pudding and black pudding.
   2 Which of these language features could be used to write a diary entry? Formal language, past tense, abbreviations, technical language, present tense, informal language. Give examples.
   3 The Wolf described himself as Grandma because ... Sort your answers into 'right', 'wrong' and 'could be' columns.

3 Starting from the answer.
   1 The answer is square. What might the question be?
   2 The Romans invaded Britain. Why?
   3 Bricks are the best material for building a house. Why?
   4 1066 was a turbulent year. Why?

4   A statement: agree or disagree.
   1   Shylock was not a villain but a victim.
   2   Every school should have its own swimming pool.
   3   All pupils should learn a foreign language.
   4   Glass is an excellent material for making a shelter.
   5   Guy Fawkes was a wicked man.
   6   The moon is a source of light.

5   An opposing viewpoint.
   1   Why would some Celts see the Roman invasion of Britain as a good thing?
   2   How might a bully justify their actions?
   3   Would you use a drug that had been tested on animals to cure a member of your family?

Understanding *how* to learn will help pupils to tackle unfamiliar tasks in school, to approach challenges in a methodical way and appreciate the different options that are available to them. When they are able to adopt such approaches in school, they will be more likely to transfer problem-solving techniques to life outside school. The skills they will require in order to help themselves with problem solving will include social ability, empathy and collaborative techniques. Chapter 4 discusses the ways in which social skills can be developed through input in the mainstream classroom.

## Bibliography

Black, P. and Wiliam, D. (1998) *Inside the Black Box: Raising standards through classroom assessment.* London: GL Assessment Limited.

Bloom, B. (1956) *Taxonomy of Educational Objectives.* Boston, MA: Allyn and Bacon (revised edition 1984 by Pearson Education).

Brown, G. and Conrad, E. (1993) *Questioning.* London: Routledge.

Cotton, K. (1988) *Instructional Reinforcement.* Portland, OR: Northwest Regional Educational Laboratory.

de Bono, E. (1985) *Six Thinking Hats: An essential approach to business management.* Boston, MA: Little, Brown and Company.

Feuerstein, R. (1999) *Mediated Learning Experience (MLE): Theoretical, psychosocial and learning implications.* Tel Aviv, Jaffa, Israel: Freund Publishing House.

Hattie, J. (2008) *Visible Learning: A synthesis of over 800 meta-analyses relating to achievement.* New York: Routledge.

Lipman, M. (1976) *Philosophy for Children*. Oxford: Basil Blackwell.

Shayer, M. and Adey, P. (1980) *Cognitive Acceleration*. London: King's College London.

Wragg E.C. and Brown G. (2001) *Questioning in the Primary School*. London and New York: RoutledgeFalmer.

# CHAPTER 4

# Social skills

Children will need social skills in order to work with and relate to others. Young children learn their social skills from their immediate family through observation and mimicry. Children's small social circles will gradually expand during their formative years to include extended family, neighbours, family friends, adults and children from play schemes and Mother and Toddler groups. When children enter school they will further extend their social networks and meet more children and adults: their peers, older children in the school, teachers, office staff, the headteacher, lunchtime supervisors, teaching assistants and other parents. Different behaviours will be required when communicating with these different groups and teaching children social conventions is part of the hidden curriculum of all schools.

Pupils with good social skills will be:

1. able to maintain friendships and relationships over the long term
2. able to cooperate and compromise
3. able to have the ability to give and take in relationships
4. comfortable in new situations
5. able to trust others and encourage others to trust them
6. able to problem solve – when social difficulties crop up, they will stand back and work out what to do rather than act impulsively without thinking of possible consequences
7. assertive when necessary and able to apologise when they know they are in the wrong.

## Developing social skills

### Model appropriate behaviour in the classroom

All children will benefit from learning about social behaviour. Recent research points to children who spend a significant amount of their free time on social media sites, experiencing a reduction in their face-to-face communication skills and so the need for social communication training in the classroom may be becoming more of a priority for schools.

The increased use of social media and an associated rise in cyber bullying is cited as a significant cause of mental distress in young people. Research into the lives of ten-to-fifteen year olds carried out by academics at the Schools and Students Health Education Unit revealed that 36 per cent of Year 8 girls and 23 per cent of Year 8 boys were sometimes or often afraid of going to school because of fears they would be bullied.

Research data shows that, between 2010 and 2014, the proportion of children aged nine to ten who have experienced some form of cyber bullying tripled and the proportion of children between thirteen and fourteen who experienced cyber bullying almost doubled (Net Children Go Mobile Project 2015).

> Be nice to people. No-one becomes successful on their own.
>
> (Rosemary Conley, health and fitness expert)

If there are disagreements in the classroom, show pupils how to compromise and how to disagree with others in a polite and measured way. Demonstrate the use of constructive and destructive criticism and the effect different types of criticism will have on others. When pupils become more aware of alternative ways to say things, their appreciation of the subtle nature of communication will be increased. Teach pupils how to be supportive of friends. To try to say something pleasant when friends do something well or offer help if they are finding a task difficult, to think about others and be aware of the effect that their behaviour has on them. Comment positively whenever pupils are seen being supportive or showing thoughtfulness towards their peers.

> If you want others to be happy, practise compassion. If you want to be happy, practise compassion.
>
> (Dalai Lama)

Pupils can work together to solve fictitious or real problems and then discuss their solutions: 'Toby finds it difficult to learn French vocabulary for tests. What should he do? Is there something we can do to help him?' 'Ruby reads texts very slowly. What strategies can we suggest that might be useful for her to try?' Encourage pupils to discuss several solutions or different interpretations of situations: stress the benefits of sharing support. Allow time for cooperative activities: individual, paired and group work in class. Working with supportive friends can make all the difference to some pupils' experience of school. 'For academically successful children, peers, especially their friends, offered practical and emotional support with school and learning that benefitted their attainment. The emotional support helped them to enjoy school and to deal with any difficulties they encountered' (DfE 2011).

Rotate pairing and groups so pupils work with peers they do not know or usually work with, distributing roles to ensure everyone is given an opportunity to lead, scribe, report back or chair the group. Group work is the perfect situation to introduce the concept of 'reading' the behaviour and body language of others. Pupils will need to be able to use and read different body language in different situations. The body language they use will be different when communicating with a younger child from the way they behave when dealing with a bully. Discuss and demonstrate the indicators about another person's feeling and emotions that can be acquired by studying their behaviour and the impression pupils create through their own body language:

- When you want to show someone you agree with what they are saying, nod slowly or mirror their body language.
- If you want to look confident, move briskly and purposefully and hold your head up.

- When you look down or slouch, you will appear under confident or awkward.
- If you are looking around, nodding quickly or tapping your fingers, the person you are speaking to will feel that you are getting bored.
- When you fold your arms across your chest, you will appear to be defensive or shy.
- If you stand with your hands on your hips or jab your finger towards someone, you will appear irritated or aggressive.

Practise active listening during group work:

- Look towards the speaker and maintain a reasonable level of eye contact.
- Make appropriate nodding or 'Uh-huh' sounds to show you are listening.
- Do not interrupt, even if it is to share a similar experience. Interrupting is a common error when listening to others and, while usually born from a desire to show empathy, it gives the wrong message to the other person and makes the interrupter appear self-centred.
- Wait until the speaker has finished before asking questions.
- Asking a question or repeating what the speaker has said in another way will reassure the person that you are interested. 'So what you are saying is …'
- Listen carefully to what other pupils have to say rather than anticipating your next input. This is another common trait in listeners that makes them appear self-centred.

Hold 'Circle Times' to encourage pupils to be open minded and to listen to the views of others. There are always several ways of looking at a situation, so encourage pupils to gather information from different sources to get a balanced overview. Pupils need to know how to express thoughts and feelings clearly without their emotions getting in the way. As adults they will need to be assertive without being aggressive or allowing others to take advantage of them. If they are unhappy about something, they need to consider what options are available to improve the situation. Stress the fact that situations are rarely hopeless and there is always something the individual can do to improve the circumstance. Discussion with others is one way to deal with choices and decisions: a problem shared is a problem halved. When problems are discussed with others, alternative solutions may become clear because of the objectivity of the other person's viewpoint.

Respect pupil difference and show you are aware of individual preferences by providing a range of learning experiences. Some individuals may enjoy working independently on projects and find it distracting to have to participate in group activities. It would be hard, if not impossible, to adhere to Gladwell's (2002) '10,000 hour rule', without being happy with one's own company. This does not necessarily mean that an individual lacks social skills or self-confidence, they simply like working by themselves and sometimes they will need that option. However, effective learners need to keep a balance between sociability and independence. They need to appreciate that they can learn from others, while still valuing time with their own thoughts.

## Model good social skills as an individual

Socially adept individuals will encourage, help, forgive, apologise, be polite and considerate. The less socially adept will mock, blame, criticise, argue, spread gossip and hold grudges. Pupils will learn more from teachers' behaviour than from teacher talk and the empathetic example of adults is essential.

Display consistent and considerate behaviour. Unpredictable adults can be hard for children to deal with and sociable individuals will always be predictable in terms of their behaviour. Be firm and fair, consistent on rules, without displaying favouritism, be seen to settle disputes, avoid confrontation and apply fair discipline. Training in appropriate social skills occurs through the constant reinforcement of the desired behaviour. When children are taught by their parents not to drop litter, they will find it an impossible habit to break. When children are taught to be kind and thoughtful towards others, it will be difficult for them to behave selfishly.

Demonstrate caring behaviour by taking an interest in pupils and asking how the hockey match went, when their father will be back from his business trip, if they were chosen for the part in the play. Very few people listen to others properly because they are too busy thinking about their next comment or how what the person is saying relates to them. Listen carefully when pupils talk and take time to get to know them better. Encourage them to come and ask for help: be approachable but give guidance rather than answers to encourage independence. Always emphasise to pupils that every day is a fresh start and a new opportunity: they should not worry about what happened yesterday but make resolutions about what is going to happen in the future.

It is worth remembering that teacher morale matters and adults in schools need to look after their own well-being. Teachers join the profession because they like children and want to do their best for them, but this is not always appreciated. Teachers will need to have self-respect in order to promote well-being in others. According to Russell Hobby from the National Association of Head Teachers, 'The idea that confident teachers are more effective seems pretty intuitive, but we've had a period of five years in which teachers have felt distrusted and undermined'.

Figures from the Department for Education published in 2015 showed that 38 per cent of teachers left the profession within a year of qualifying: 43,440 state school teachers left the profession in 2012, 45,640 in 2013 and 49,120 in 2015. Improving schools as places of learning for pupils will improve schools as places of teaching for teachers.

## Establish a whole school approach

Work with parents. The well-being of children is a shared responsibility and schools need to work closely with parents to achieve continuity of care. Good home–school links will ensure the school is aware of any situation at home that may impinge on the pupil's behaviour or performance in the classroom, and that the family knows of any situations in school that may be provoking unexpected reactions from the pupil at home.

Ensure mentoring systems are in place to support pupils who are new to the school or experiencing difficulties. Support may need to be targeted towards points of transition when pupils may be particularly vulnerable. Older pupils could be trained as mentors to help settle disputes between younger children.

The support and interest of adults in school can make a huge difference to pupils' self-confidence. When they receive consideration and kindness, they will be more likely to show consideration and kindness to others. Such behaviour will make them more popular, which in turn will help them to understand the value of altruistic behaviour.

Pupils will learn social skills from involvement with groups outside school, voluntary work and work experience. Schools need to act as a bridge into such associations, creating links and opportunities for pupils.

Pupils will gain experience of mixing socially with a wider group in terms of age, gender and social class through Outward Bound, the Duke of Edinburgh Award Scheme or youth groups, charitable bodies, sports clubs and church associations.

Develop inter-school links to share facilities, resources and extend friendship groups through joint sport, drama and music events, mentoring schemes and integrated clubs and societies. Cooperation between schools will be more productive than competition.

## Wider social skills can be encouraged through community service

Community service can help pupils to develop empathic attitudes and help them to understand the lives of others, why they might behave as they do and what is motivating them. It is worth pointing out that for a healthy attitude to life, pupils need to be aware of those people who do not have their advantages, rather than look to others who seem to have more. Happiness is to be found within themselves, rather than within life experiences. Human beings adapt quickly to new situations and the realisation of long-held dreams (getting into the desired university, going out with that special boy, possessing a new car or having holidays of a lifetime every six months) will only reduce the satisfaction gained from previous simpler pleasures. When it is possible to travel across the world to exotic locations, the fun of caravanning in the Isle of Wight may diminish but, over time, the delights of a fortnight in the Maldives will fade and new, more exciting destinations craved.

Lasting personal satisfaction and happiness can be created by helping others who are less fortunate rather than feeling jealous of those who do well at school, seem more attractive or appear luckier. Adults cannot always have the job, holiday or house they would like, but are certain to have more than many people they know. Happiness is a luxury of the developed world, in many societies the population is too busy surviving and trying to raise their family safely to think about being happy.

Pupils can access numerous opportunities for voluntary work through organisations outside of school: helping younger children at the local pre-school group or nursery; volunteering at church or local youth groups; becoming involved with the running of Brownies, Scouts, Guides or Sea Cadets; or visiting elderly people and gardening or shopping for them. Schools themselves can provide a wealth of opportunities for volunteering: hearing younger children read; helping with the running of sports groups, school councils, art and drama clubs; or through mentoring and prefect systems. Such activities will help to provide a secure foundation for pupils' future parenting skills.

When pupils are involved in voluntary work, it will keep their own problems in perspective and help them to feel better about themselves. When they understand that they can play a useful role in society and are needed by others, their self-confidence will increase and they will feel more comfortable in social situations.

Pupils could organise charity events such as book, cake, toy and car boot sales, charity runs, sponsored silences, concerts and craft fairs to support charities of their choice. Individual pupils could research different charities, contacting the association's head office, collecting literature about their work and giving talks in assembly, PHSE lessons or form time. Reaching out to different groups will necessitate pupils negotiating and collaborating with others, widening their social circles and provide positive reinforcement for their self-worth.

Work experience and Saturday jobs will provide a taste of what life can be like for adults. When pupils have experienced work as a shop assistant, a waitress or a domestic assistant in a hotel, they will appreciate the pressure some adults experience at work and be less likely to treat people in a high-handed way. A Saturday job or holiday work in a bar, local shop or restaurant may be motivating or provide a dose of reality. Would you like this job on a permanent basis? Do you need to consider your behaviour towards bar, restaurant or shop staff when you go out with friends? Do you need to think about what you would like to do and, perhaps more importantly, what you would not like to do in the future?

When pupils have good social skills, they will have high levels of self-confidence. They will enjoy the company of others and feel able to demonstrate kind and caring behaviour. The feedback they get from their social interaction will be positive. They will know that others like them and value their company. When children feel good about themselves, they will feel secure and be willing to try new activities, find it easier to bounce back from disappointment and be more willing to accept frustration as part of life and move on from failure. Chapter 5 discusses the importance of pupils' self-confidence for the development of their happiness and well-being.

## References

DfE (2011) *Performing Against the Odds: Developmental trajectories of children in the EPPSE 3–16 study*. DFE-RR128.

Gladwell, M. (2002) The talent myth. *The New Yorker*, 22 July.

Mascheroni, G. and Cuman, A. (2014) *Net Children Go Mobile*. Milan: EDUCatt.

Net Children Go Mobile Project (2015) *Net Children Go Mobile*. Milan: EDUCatt.

# CHAPTER 5

# Self-confidence

Pupils' levels of self-confidence will be linked to self-discipline, emotional regulation, positivity, ability to deal with failure and disappointment, persistence and self-motivation. These skills are developed through personal relationships and social interaction. The fundamental relationship for a child being the one that exists between themselves and their parents or carers. The 'Promoting children and young people's mental health and well being' report was published by Public Health England and the Children and Young People's Mental Health Coalition in 2015. According to the report, in an average class of thirty fifteen year olds, ten pupils will have seen their parents separate or divorce. There have been significant changes over recent years in the structure of the modern family. One in three people in the UK today is a step-parent, step-child, adult step-child, step-sibling or step-grandparent. Living within a traditional family of mother, father and siblings is no longer the normal experience of significant numbers of children and young people. 'The experience of emotionally and practically supportive relationships with parents, peers, friends and significant others nurture[s] children's self perceptions, sense of self efficacy and effective learning strategies, which help them to become active agents in their learning discourse' (DfE 2011).

## The role played by parents

Young children develop their self-image through interaction with the significant others in their lives. Do the children feel they are seen to be interesting, good company and deserving of unconditional love?

Children will develop into emotionally stable adults when they are listened to, given affection and understanding, with adults responding to and taking action on their behalf over any concerns and worries. Layard and Clark (2015) state: 'The best protection against mental illness is positive parenting – a harmonious relationship with at least one adult who is totally committed, dependable and appreciative.'

There has been a shift during the past thirty years from child care within the home to child care provided privately or by the state. Many young couples lack direct experience of small children. They may not live near their extended family and have not seen relatives coping with babies and toddlers. They may be only children or from small families themselves with little experience of responsibility for siblings or cousins. They may be unaware of how small children behave and vulnerable to suggestion from peers, magazines, health professionals or the internet. Parents may be inclined to follow the advice of 'experts' rather than their own instincts. However, the internet cannot appreciate an individual child's needs or the circumstances of their family, and the advice of friends may be tinged with their own personal anxieties, jealousy or prejudices.

Some parents will feel pre-school care is a way to give their child a head start in the educational race and may not appreciate that they will have a greater invested interest in their child than staff working in a pre-school provision. Parents are able to provide the individually tailored care that is appropriate for the current needs and interests of their own child. When young children are able to forge strong emotional bonds with their parents from an early age, these bonds will provide a source of strength and security for the rest of their lives. Education is important, but life goes on for a long time after school and a wide range of social and emotional skills are essential for adult happiness.

Human beings are born, go to school, get a job, move house, form relationships, have a family, go on holidays, get old and die. That is the pattern of life. The main gifts parents can pass on to their children are the attributes of kindness, empathy, a sense of right and wrong, an enthusiasm for life, and physical and mental health. Such attributes will be cultivated when parents invest time, energy and love in raising their children.

According to Education Secretary Nicky Morgan, the current government aims to 'Encourage more schools to offer nursery provision and extend that provision from 8am to 6pm. Help schools to offer affordable after-school and holiday care, either alone or working with private or voluntary providers.'

An increase in the provision of free child care, an extension in the hours of such provision and a reduction in children's entitlement to holiday demonstrates clearly a total lack of appreciation of the importance of parents and family to a child's development. In the General Election of May 2015, all major parties pledged to extend free child care for three and four year olds: the Conservative Party offering thirty hours, the Labour Party twenty-five hours and the Liberal Democrats twenty hours of child care to all parents of two-to-four year olds and to working parents when their babies are nine months old.

The priority for schools and nurseries providing pre-school care must be to look after and cater for the children's needs and not to provide a convenient and cheap childminding service. While some early education provisions are excellent, they are not required by all families and are not suitable for everyone. All young children have different individual needs: a nursery placement may be appropriate for one child but will not be a substitute for one-to-one care with a familiar adult for another.

In order for children to develop secure 'attachment', research points to the need for children under two or three years of age to have one-to-one care with a consistent figure: a parent, grandparent or dedicated child minder. The mother/child attachment theory originates with the work of John Bowlby in the 1940s. Bowlby worked as a psychiatrist in a Child Guidance Clinic in London, where he treated emotionally disturbed children. Bowlby (1944) developed his attachment theory in recognition of the importance of mother/child bonding for the children's social, emotional and cognitive development and the success of their future relationships.

The majority of time the child spends in interaction in a nursery setting will be with other young children. This will offer a less effective input in, for example, the development of language, than if the child were interacting on a one-to-one basis with a familiar adult. There will be numerous small group opportunities designed to support language development in nurseries but many children will prefer to spend their time with their peers and young children do not always provide good linguistic models. While all nurseries will offer opportunities to develop language through exposure to books, such opportunities tend to occur in group settings, so the children do not always benefit individually. The book being read may be about a topic outside the child's personal experience, they may not understand the vocabulary, they may want to ask questions but not have the opportunity, they may not have enough time to look at the pictures, be unable to see the pictures clearly or to have time to discuss links between the story and their own lives.

Care for young children in nurseries is a case of swings and roundabouts. The child will gain social experience from interaction with other children and adults but lose the opportunity for personalised interaction with a familiar adult. Nursery care cannot be a replacement for family life. Workers in the UK do not have to work more than 48 hours a week, unless they choose to. This law is referred to as the 'working time directive' or 'working time regulations'. Are there limitations on the number of hours children can attend a nursery? Do pre-school children benefit from a fifty-hour week in nursery care? If travel time is added to the time spent in the nursery, some children's whole waking day will be spent outside the family home. All workers have, from the first day of employment, the right to several weeks' paid holiday per year. Do babies and young children share this right?

When parents spend limited amounts of time with their children, how valued will the children feel? How will they feel towards their parents and how strong will the emotional bonds be within the family? Will those children care about the wishes of their parents in fifty years time when the parents are old and vulnerable? Are children being set a good example of how to treat less powerful members of their immediate family, extended family or society in general? 'All small exchanges between parent and child have an emotional subtext and, in the repetition of these messages over the years, children form the core of their emotional outlook and capabilities' (Goleman 1996).

If parents are to understand their children, they need to be involved in their daily life. When parents spend time with their children, they will develop a better understanding of the children's interests, strengths, things that are worrying them and the activities that they enjoy. This will help parents to support the children: 'No need to worry about that. You say that you are no good at reading, but can you remember when Grandad first took you swimming and you couldn't swim a stroke, but then after a few weeks you got really good. Reading is exactly the same, it is difficult at first, but then you practise and you get better.'

Rather than taking their children to specialist classes, parents could spend time playing with them, taking them to the playground, for a bike ride, swimming or playing football in the garden. Young children do not need football, cricket or swimming lessons, they need to have fun. Children need to enjoy the company of those who care most about them: parents, siblings, grandparents, their extended family and family friends.

Parents should take an interest in their children's schools: attending parents' evenings, fundraising events, plays, school fairs, concerts, assemblies, sports days and information evenings. Parents need to listen to their children and, if appropriate, speak up on their behalf. If they are unhappy, being bullied (by children or teachers) or are anxious in any way, the child needs to know their parents will listen to and support them and that the school will be made aware of the problem. Emphasise to the children that their best is always going to be good enough and reassure them that parental love is unconditional. 'Do your best and no-one can ask for more' should be a mantra for all parents.

# Developing pupils' self-confidence in schools

Schools need to complement children's social and emotional experiences in order to support the development of their self-confidence.

## Controlling negative emotions

Emotional regulation refers to an individual's ability to manage their emotions and stay calm when they experience stress or are put under pressure. When pupils have problems controlling their temper, adults need to suggest anger management strategies, ways of self-calming and demonstrate how to discuss solutions to problems.

Teach pupils to anticipate personal anger triggers and to put avoidance strategies into place early in the cycle of anger. Discuss self-calming strategies, always emphasising the need to think before acting. When pupils begin to feel irritated, show them how to distract themselves with another activity: take some time out, walk away from the situation, run up and down the stairs, or play a game of football to burn off angry feelings.

When pupils argue with friends, encourage each individual to look at the disagreement from the friend's point of view and discuss the concept of compromise. Help them to talk about problems calmly and think about possible solutions, to consider the consequences of different solutions and try the action plan that seems best. The way in which we perceive situations will affect the way we feel, so show pupils how to step away, to try to view the situation objectively and to see events for what they really are. There are always two points of view in an argument and the friend might be feeling ill, tired or worried about something: stress the concept of being generous and giving others the benefit of the doubt. Explain that it is not always a good idea to handle problems immediately and that sometimes it can be better to listen and watch rather than do. Many difficult situations will solve themselves given time or more suitable solutions worked out away from the heat of the moment.

Emotion and upset need to be experienced and dealt with, but pupils should be encouraged not to get stuck with a grievance and be provided with a plan of action to overcome any lingering resentment and avoid cycles of blame.

There is usually something that can be done to make a situation better. Pupils should focus on how to improve a situation, rather than think about how hopeless everything is and wonder why awful things always happen to them. Point out that those situations outside the pupil's immediate control – the weather, international politics or the form of the national cricket team – can be ignored and should not be worried about.

Explain that emotions can get in the way of achievement. Pupils who are anxious, angry or depressed will find it harder to learn. Stress that the pupil's level of physical health will affect their mental well-being, so they should try to get enough sleep, to eat properly and take adequate exercise.

No matter what has gone before, every day should be seen as a fresh start and a new opportunity for the pupil.

## Developing positivity

To develop positive thinking, suggest pupils make comparisons with their own previous efforts and not those of their peers. 'I got 45 per cent last time, now I'm going to aim for a mark of over 50 per cent' being more appropriate than, 'I failed last time but this time I'm going to get at least 95 per cent and beat Toby'. A realistic approach means that pupils are less likely to be disappointed. They can get closer to a target grade even if they don't quite achieve it. Pupils with realistic optimism will be more likely to bounce back from disappointment and try again.

Give feedback that recognises effort. 'Well done, all your hard work is really paying off.' 'I know this topic is hard to understand when you haven't done it at GCSE but I can see you're trying. Keep asking questions whenever you are uncertain.' 'Thank you for helping your group to understand this section. You explained it very well.' Feedback to parents in reports should also include comments about effort, determination and other positive personality traits.

Although no one can be marvellous at everything, encourage pupils to visualise good things happening and not to be overly pessimistic.

Pupils with a pessimistic outlook will assume that everything will go wrong and be reluctant to try anything new because they 'know' that it won't be worth it and they are certain to fail.

Children learn through imitation and it is important that when adults come up against problems, they model optimistic behaviour and talk about ways to get around the difficulty. This will demonstrate to pupils that adults do not give up, they simply adapt their strategies. 'What can we do that we haven't already tried?' 'I wonder who is best to ask for help.' 'Is there another way to solve this? Am missing something obvious?'

Being friends with positive people is less draining than mixing with those who always see the negative side of life. If pupils are feeling upset or disappointed, encourage them to seek out positive friends for support.

Suggest pupils use self-talk. 'Never mind, worse things happen at sea.' 'Oh well, maybe we'll have better luck next time.' 'As my Granny used to say, nothing ventured, nothing gained.' Such expressions can be a jokey way of dealing with disappointment, and sometimes self-talk can be enough to enable the individual to continue with their effort.

Remind pupils that life is a marathon, not a sprint. Young people have a lot of time to get things right and should think about and judge their performance over the long term: weeks rather than days and months rather than weeks.

## Dealing with failure and disappointment

It is important that pupils are able to deal appropriately with disappointment. Suggest pupils take a small-step approach towards a target in order to reduce the impact of any failure. Provide the pupil with evidence of progress by recording the steps they have already made.

Minimise stress by gradually increasing pupils' exposure to unfamiliar situations and helping them to step slightly outside their comfort zone. Help pupils during periods of transition and scaffold appropriate coping strategies, reminding them not to set wildly unrealistic expectations or be too hard on themselves.

Teach pupils how to tolerate not knowing, and reassure them that uncertainty or not understanding quite what you have to do is all part of the learning process. Ensure that feedback is designed to help pupils to improve. Good feedback should enable pupils to see errors as opportunities to learn.

> Celebrate mistakes. You can always learn much more from your mistakes than your successes.
>
> (James Dyson, Founder of Dyson)

If a sense of fun and pleasure in learning is maintained, learning is less likely to become a chore or be perceived as threatening and uncomfortable. Celebrate a wide variety of achievements. Adults in the school can contribute to a 'What I am most proud of' display. I completed a half marathon, passed my driving test, joined a choir, flew for the first time, joined Weight Watchers, gave a speech at my son's wedding or passed my Maths GCSE at thirty-five years of age.

Give alternative prizes at School Prize-Giving to show how the school community values a wide range of achievement and personal attributes. Create displays of work, struggles and successes, showing the lives of individuals who experienced failure, survived extreme experience or overcome adversity. Mount displays of former pupils, their achievements and the characteristics that enabled them to succeed.

> I haven't failed: I've just found 10,000 ways that won't work.
>
> (Thomas Edison, inventor and businessman)

Set work that provides a balance between challenge and achievability, incorporating a few activities that can be failed. Experiencing failure is a particularly important for those pupils who find everything in school easy. No one becomes an expert without learning from errors.

The term 'resilience' refers to the individual's ability to deal appropriately with stress and adversity. Key factors in the development of resilience include possessing a positive outlook and maintaining a sense of humour. Research by the French psychologist Boris Cyrulnik (2011) has shown that when people view adversity as a challenging, yet worthwhile, experience, they are able to see how difficult experiences might turn out to be for the best in the future. Resilient individuals can develop inner strength through facing up to and dealing with adversity.

Some pupils will be able to coast through school with little experience of failure, while others will experience regular small setbacks and embarrassments. One advantage for pupils with mild specific learning difficulties is that they will be familiar with feelings of foolishness and disappointment, and therefore are in a perfect position to develop personal resilience.

> I kept expecting to fail. Not being afraid of failing has been a useful skill. As an actor, you can't be fazed by failure.
>
> (Cerrie Burnel, actress, TV presenter and dyslexic)

When a pupil experiences failure, they will become more empathetic and forgiving of the mistakes that others make. Possessing a sympathetic attitude will make pupils more popular and help them to understand that as everyone makes mistakes sometimes, there is no need to be overly self-critical.

If your first failure appears significant (failing your driving lesson, failing to get the job of your dreams or to get into your university of choice), your disappointment may be magnified out of all proportion. Success that comes easily to an individual can reduce their determination and drive and they may lack staying power when things go wrong.

Encourage pupils to be prepared to adapt their ambitions. Many adults follow satisfying alternative career paths and achieve personal contentment through meandering, less obvious routes that enrich their lives and make them more interesting people. Suggest that pupils should be flexible about their ambitions and realistic about personal limitations, rather than push themselves to achieve a perfectionist ideal. Failure can hurt at first but, when dealt with positively, will make the individual stronger.

## Encouraging pupils to be brave

The fear of looking silly can stop pupils from trying, but knowing that everyone makes mistakes and that it isn't disastrous will help them to take risks. Henry Ford's first business adventure, the Detroit Automobile Company, collapsed, as did his second business venture, but his third company, The Ford Motor Company, became a worldwide success.

> Anyone who has never made a mistake has never tried anything new.
>
> (Albert Einstein)

If pupils are anxious about appearing foolish, ask them to take time and analyse what they are really worried about. What is the worst that could happen? Will this matter next week? Next year? Who would remember it apart from you?

Suggest pupils share concerns with others: a problem shared is a problem halved. Friends and family may be able to rationalise pupils' anxieties, put worries into perspective or present possible solutions to problems that they had not considered previously.

Encourage pupils not to take themselves too seriously and to laugh at their mistakes. If they take themselves seriously, they will be more likely to take offence from any perceived criticism, become defensive, not listen to the opinions of others or learn from their mistakes.

Teach pupils to consider the advantages of being brave. Many pupils will stay in friendships or stick with unsuitable subject choices because they are frightened of change. Lots of situations may feel uncomfortable at first, but, after a while, turn out to be for the best. Pupils should not confuse fear that keeps them safe with fear that stops them from doing what they want to do.

> The worst regret in life is not failing at something, but not having tried in the first place and never knowing what might have been.
>
> (Terry Venables, footballer)

Offer pupils regular opportunities to perform and display alternative talents: conjuring tricks, playing the bagpipes, Irish dancing, barber shop singing, parkour or street dance routines. Performing in front of peers can be difficult, but will boost confidence and be worth a bout of pre-performance nerves.

Teach pupils to be flexible, open-minded, responsive to situations, to develop a 'nothing ventured, nothing gained' attitude, to seize new opportunities and, if opportunities don't arise, to create them.

It may be difficult for the pupil to avoid negativity from all of their acquaintances, but pessimistic peers can be draining. Suggest it might be easier for them to discuss personal ambitions with those family members and friends who will be realistic, but also supportive and positive.

> Keep away from people who try to belittle your ambitions. Small people always do that but the really great ones make you feel that you, too, can become great.
>
> (Mark Twain, author)

## Developing persistence

Anders Ericsson, a Swedish psychologist, looked at the effect of practise on the performance of violinists from the Berlin Academy of Music. The violinists were put into groups: world-class soloists, professional musicians and music teachers. By the age of twenty, the three groups had practised for 10,000, 8,000 hours and 4,000 hours respectively. None of the professional violinists had practised for less than 8,000 hours. Within the top two groups, talent was irrelevant; it was hard work that had produced results.

The value of effort is discussed in Malcolm Gladwell's book *Outliers* (2008). Gladwell claims that successful individuals owe their success to continued effort, practising and refining their skills over a period of at least 10,000 hours. He quotes numerous examples of such dedication, including The Beatles, one of the most famous pop group of the 1960s. Prior to achieving international fame, The Beatles spent hours honing their musical skills by playing in night clubs in Germany. By 1962, they were playing eight hours per day, seven days per week and, by 1964, when they became international stars, they had performed together over 1,200 times.

> If you knew how much work went into it, you wouldn't call it genius.
>
> (Michelangelo, talking about the Sistine Chapel ceiling)

Learning isn't meant to be easy. Pupils should be taught to work steadily, at their own pace and not to expect instant results. Musicians, sportsmen and women and entrepreneurs do not expect immediate reward, but know they must delay gratification for some future date. Children who can demonstrate self-discipline are more likely to attend school regularly, do homework conscientiously, go to bed at a reasonable hour and revise rather than watch TV or play computer games. The long-term benefits of delayed gratification and the fact that willpower is a skill that everyone can develop should be discussed with pupils. Walter Mischel's famous 'marshmallow' experiment with pre-school children at Stanford University in the 1960s could be used as an introduction to discussion. The group of children in the experiment (Mischel *et al.* 1989) were presented with one marshmallow and told that if they could wait to eat it until the adult returned from another room, they would be given a second marshmallow. When the same children were tracked down as adolescents in the 1980s/1990s, those who had resisted the temptation to eat the first marshmallow were found to be more self-assertive, socially competent, self-reliant, calmer, resilient and had better academic results than the second group.

## Developing motivation

It is important that pupils develop intrinsic motivation rather than be dependent on external pressure. It is preferable for the pupil to say 'I'm planning to work really hard in English because I need to get a "C" for my college course', rather than a teacher saying 'You'll never get a decent job if you don't revise core subjects'. The development of intrinsic motivation and self-control is one of the long-term aims of parenting: young children being steered towards acceptable behaviour with an emphasis on creating an internal moral code. 'Be kind. That hurt Theo and you wouldn't like it if he pinched you', rather than 'If I see you hit Theo again, I'll smack you, you naughty boy'. It is essential that pupils are able to motivate themselves if they are to have autonomy in their lives.

Choice is a motivating force. Learners will become more involved when they have a degree of control over the learning process and will appreciate having the opportunity to take decisions about their learning. Choice in the classroom can mean quite minor adaptations: instead of always writing up notes in essay form, create a series of explanatory diagrams or an annotated timeline, write an entry for a diary, draw a cartoon sequence, compose a series of letters between individuals, organise a class debate or give a presentation with sets of handouts.

Give opportunities in the classroom to accommodate different learning styles. Recognising pupils' learning preferences can help teachers to identify those approaches to teaching and learning that will satisfy individual pupils' needs. Does the pupil enjoy working alone because they have specialist knowledge of that module or an all-absorbing interest in a topic? Are they happy to learn in any subject as long as they can work alongside their friends? Drama and role play might not be the teaching approach of choice for many teachers, but can be an effective way for some pupils to learn. Providing a variety of 'hands-on' learning opportunities (practical projects, theatre trips, local visits, work experience and talks and demonstrations from outside experts) will ensure lessons are of interest to those pupils who learn through practical participation and activity. This group of pupils can be learners whose needs are often overlooked in the classroom.

> I didn't get here by dreaming or thinking about it. I got here by doing it.
>
> (Estée Lauder, businesswoman)

Provide a supportive and encouraging environment where pupils feel that their ideas matter. They don't always need to be right, but can feel free to ask questions and learn through discussion. When pupils experience an environment that fosters self-reliance and independence, they will be more willing to take risks. Learners who are relaxed and calm are better placed to absorb knowledge and develop skills.

Tension and anxiety will be reduced when a non-threatening environment exists in the classroom and all mistakes are seen as learning opportunities. Fear, anxiety, stress and anger are all negative factors that will adversely affect pupils' learning.

Identify the everyday relevance of the topic or the learning activity to ensure pupils appreciate how the skills they are acquiring are applicable to real-life situations. Linking classroom work to the real world will help pupils to develop the life skills of problem solving and reasoning. For suggestions to encourage pupil motivation, see Section IV, pupil advice sheet: 'How to motivate yourself'.

## Increasing self-confidence to feed into self-respect

Pupils need to develop self-respect in order to make progress. Children will learn to respect others when they have been shown kindness and understanding themselves. When a pupil is content and happy, they will be less likely to need to upset others.

> Respect yourself and others will respect you.
>
> (Confucius)

While parenting is pivotal to the development of the child's well-being, adults in school can offer additional supporting and validating roles. When a child feels listened to and appreciated, they are more likely to develop confidence. Children who do not feel worthy of respect will seek validation from their peers and be more susceptible to self-doubt. When a child receives adequate attention and affection, they will not be overly concerned about the opinions other pupils hold about them. They will be mentally stronger and less likely to be vulnerable to suggestions from those peers they would like to impress. If they try to befriend someone, but the other person does not reciprocate, they will move on and let the apparent slight go. Children with adequate levels of confidence will be less likely to become victims of bullying and more likely to report any verbal or physical abuse. They will not see bullying behaviour as something that they have deserved.

My reasons for choosing these best teachers are almost non-educational, as ludicrous as that sounds … They were the first teachers who actually listened to us – that's how we all felt and that's why we still speak of them in such fond terms.

(Greg Davies, actor and comedian)

If an individual is not developing self-respect within school, help them to look for positive validation outside school, such as Scouts, Guides, church associations, sports clubs, choirs, amateur dramatics, voluntary or community groups. *Appreciation and confirmation from such sources will give a child confidence, no matter how different they feel from their peer group within school.*

Give pupils responsibilities. Appoint class monitors and council reps, develop a school prefect system, encourage older pupils to run clubs for younger children, to organise charity events within the school, to coach junior teams or hear younger pupils read. Older pupils could help teaching staff tutor younger pupils in Homework Clubs or Subject Surgeries. Respect from younger children can boost the self-esteem of older pupils.

Give pupils responsibility for school pets or school garden. Caring for pets will give pupils a sense of responsibility, compassion and a 'friend' to confide in. Ask pupils to design the garden, choose which plants to put where and to decide what kind of fruit and vegetables to grow. The introduction of gardens and nature areas to school sites as places for pupils to spend their free time or to use as a work base will provide attractive connections with the natural world. When pupils can have an alternative learning experience in outdoor locations and are able to enjoy spending time in the natural world through residentials and expeditions to rural or coastal settings, trips to local parks or nature trails, camping weekends and field trips, a lifelong interest in the outdoors may be sparked.

As a child, my father often used to take me climbing on the small sea cliffs on the Isle of Wight. For me it was such a powerful connection with him and the natural world.

(Bear Grylls, explorer and TV presenter)

## The role to be played by adult mentors

Much of the behaviour exhibited by children in modern society (bullying, risk taking, self-harm, low self-esteem and body image problems) mirror the behaviours traditionally associated with children in care. This would suggest that some of the pupils' problems may have roots in the evolution of the modern family. One person in every three in the UK is a step-parent, step-child, step-sibling or step-grandparent. The International Resilience Project of 1997, which surveyed 600 eleven year olds, described the three adversities most commonly reported by the children as being the death of a parent or grandparent, divorce and parental separation. A child may experience attachment problems when living in a family with a step-parent and step-siblings. It can be hard for children to cope with feelings of jealousy towards their own brothers and sisters in a traditional two-parent family. These feelings become increasingly complicated when living with a parent, step-parent and step-siblings, and knowing that your other parent is living with another step-parent and your other siblings or step-siblings.

In many families, both parents will work outside the home and the child will be placed in Before and After School 'wrap around care' and/or Homework, Breakfast and Holiday clubs. The amount of time children spend with their parents and family may be limited, and the time parents can devote to family life restricted. Teachers and other adults in school can compensate to some extent with research consistently demonstrating the importance of positive relationships between teachers and pupils. Pupils who enjoy a sense of affiliation to the adults in their school are more likely to feel included, accepted, respected and supported. The influence of such mentors in valuing and affirming the pupil as a person and communicating high expectations of what they might achieve can make all the difference to a young person's self-belief. It is impossible to underestimate the effect that the genuine interest of a teacher can have on a pupil's life. Interest and mentoring from specific members of staff may be of particular importance to those pupils who are not academic in a traditional sense or non-conformist in their outlook.

Karen Howell, the art teacher, was my saviour. I already knew I wanted to act and sing when I left school and she was probably the only person who didn't scoff at my ambition.

(Toyah Willcox, singer and actress)

He was nice, you know? He cared about you outside of lessons. He was interested in the lives of his pupils and interested in our thoughts. He understood that the role of the teacher isn't just to do with academics.

(Matt Lucas, comedian)

It's not an exaggeration to say that the start of everything I do now was thanks to James. James Morwood was immensely encouraging.

(Richard Curtis, screenwriter and film-maker)

I had a lot of great teachers, but Mr Lamont and Mr Evans were the ones who stood out for me: they were the ones who listened to me and encouraged me.

(Greg Davies, actor and comedian)

You felt that she really listened and understood, and that was so reassuring. Reassurance, I think, is the key to a good teacher, along with patience, quiet intelligence and the ability to instil confidence in children.

(Kay Burley, TV newsreader and presenter)

What made him the best teacher was the personal touch, the encouragement along the way.

(Frank Lampard, footballer)

I was a shy and portly child and Mrs Baker, who taught Art, took me under her wing and encouraged me. You expect teachers to encourage you but I found that many of them took away my self-confidence.

(Jasper Conran, designer)

I took to his teaching style and Mr McWhinnie nurtured and encouraged me. He was incredibly involved and passionate and his great gift as a teacher was that he took us all seriously.

(Monty Don, TV gardener)

What made Mr Ray so special was that his lessons were consistently interesting and he seemed genuinely interested in us. When I was very young, he made me believe in myself.

(Emma Thompson, actress)

She made me, and everyone in the class, feel special.

(Joanna Trollope, novelist)

She was the only one to see I had a talent for art and I wonder if things would have been different if she'd taught me at secondary school. She might have said: 'If you work a little harder at Maths and History and get some good Highers, you could go to the Glasgow School of Art.' In fact, nobody suggested that to me at all.

(Midge Ure, musician)

Both teachers had a wonderful ability to instil confidence in their pupils. Confidence is a huge part of childhood. Confidence has such a big impact on someone's life and it can dictate what they go on to do – or not to do – beyond education.

(Jessica Ennis-Hill, athlete)

She understood every child in the class and showed me that teaching was all about caring for children and bringing them forward, not just pushing facts into them.

(Maeve Binchy, novelist)

Mentoring figures could be adults at the pupils' schools, relatives or family friends from a child's extended family, or individuals from outside school: sports clubs, church associations, local choirs and dance or drama groups. It is important for adults to remember that, while they can play a positive role in a pupil's development, the opposite can also be true.

I remember the Headteacher saying I'd never make anything of myself in front of the whole school. My ability to learn in school had been pretty much crushed out of me quite young.

(Jack Dee, comedian)

Mr Lejeune believed in me and that gave me fantastic confidence. He told me I was funny and that I had a good sense of humour. Later on, another teacher told me: 'You will never be funny. You have to be clever to be funny.' That stuck with me.

(Tim Healy, actor and comedian)

When children have good levels of confidence and understand how to tackle problems and challenges, they are more likely to be motivated to accept challenges, try new activities, think laterally and be willing to make errors. They will understand that mistakes are not important. If they make a mistake, it is not the end of the world and that it is through making errors and taking risks that new ideas will develop. Chapter 6 discusses the development of creativity in mainstream education and how a creative approach in lessons can make teaching and learning more appealing to all.

## References

Bowlby, J. (1944) Forty-four juvenile thieves: Their characters and home life. *International Journal of Psychoanalysis*, 25, 19–52.

Cyrulnik, B. (2011) *Resilience: How your inner strength can set you free from the past.* London: Penguin.

DfE (2011) *Performing Against the Odds: Developmental trajectories of children in the EPPSE 3-16 study.* DFE-RR128.

Gladwell, M. (2008) *Outliers.* Boston, MA: Little, Brown and Company.

Goleman, D. (1996) *Emotional Intelligence: Why it can matter more than IQ.* London: Bloomsbury Publishing.

Layard, R. and Clark, D. (2015) *Thrive: The power of evidence-based psychological therapies.* London: Penguin.

Mischel, W., Shoda, Y. and Rodriguzez, M.L. (1989) Delay of gratification in children. *Science*, 244: 933–8.

# CHAPTER 6

# Creativity

An individual's level of creativity relates to their ability to generate new ideas, problem solve and deal with novel situations. When a creative teaching approach is employed, teaching and learning will become more interesting because of the shift in emphasis from the regurgitation of given information to the consideration of new ideas and solutions. The inclusion of creative activities in subject lessons will increase pupil involvement, giving pupils an opportunity to step outside the usual classroom routines.

## Key point

When alternative skills are called for in a lesson rather than good memory, high levels of concentration and ability to process information at speed, a larger number of pupils will be given chances to succeed.

Creative thinking can be fostered through teaching approaches that:

1 promote curiosity
2 encourage pupils to ask questions
3 focus on the development of different types of thinking skills
4 provide a supportive and inclusive environment
5 maintain a flexible approach to learning
6 use a variety of teaching methods
7 include problem solving, case studies and enquiry tasks in lessons.

It is not the strongest of the species that survive, nor the most intelligent, but the most responsive to change.

(Charles Darwin, scientist)

The more obvious opportunities for pupils to be creative in schools through Drama, Art, Dance and Music are increasingly limited as a result of a focus on academic subjects and preparation for assessment and testing. Concentrating on a narrow set of academic skills within an overloaded curriculum will limit the time available to promote curiosity, inspiration, reflection, imagination and innovation. When pupils take eleven or twelve GCSEs, they will have less time available to reflect on their learning. There are better ways to challenge pupils than entering them for more exams.

When pupils lack creative experience, they will return to tried and tested ways of working and find it difficult to engage in speculation or 'thinking outside the box'. There is a pressing need for innovative solutions to environmental, political and social problems, and so creative thinking is a vital area for educational focus. Pupils will need to deal with situations in the future that currently cannot be anticipated or imagined. The danger exists that when the 'exam intelligent' rise to positions of authority and power, they will function well in routine problem solving, but may not have the ability to react appropriately if originality is required.

## Strategies to develop creativity in the mainstream situation

### 1 Promote curiosity

The danger exists that when pupils lack curiosity, they will become passive learners and accept whatever they are told without question.

I have no special talent. I am only passionately curious.

(Albert Einstein)

The more curious the pupils are, the more creative they will be. Curious pupils will continue to be motivated to learn, to ask questions, to research and to read around subjects. Model inquisitive behaviour: 'I don't know why that happened, but it is certainly interesting. I'll ask Mrs Parrish if she has come across that before.'

Look up information in front of pupils and wonder aloud about the facts. This can add further reassurance that it is quite acceptable to admit to limited knowledge. Pupils may be tempted to always pretend they know information when they do not. If this sort of attitude is taken into adult life, it can lead to decisions being made on flimsy evidence merely because an individual is too ashamed to admit they do not know or understand the facts.

Use subjects or topics the pupils are interested in: 'Who did he play for before he transferred to Madrid?' 'Which is the longest river in Europe?' 'I wonder how Nether Wallop got its name.' 'Where did he go to school? Was that his first job when he left school?'

Encourage pupils to see familiar places and objects in different ways and link topics to the local area: geographical features, places of worship, architecture, industrial sites, and parks and woodland. Go on trips of discovery within the locality: to identify trees in the park, or to record the names on gravestones in the churchyard or the makes of cars in a nearby street. Do any patterns emerge? Are there horse chestnut trees in the park but no conifers? Why might that be? Do the same family names appear on the gravestones in the cemetery? Which names appear on the war memorial? Are there pupils in the school who share those surnames? Are there certain types of cars parked in different roads around the school? Which types of car are in different streets? Why might that be? Demonstrate how to use your powers of observation to support curiosity. 'I wonder why they …' 'Did you notice …?' 'Why did that happen …?'

Involve the local community. Establish contacts with local individuals, clubs and societies: businessmen/women and entrepreneurs, theatres, choirs, libraries, clubs, museums and retirement groups. Use these contacts to give talks, to provide information, to support individual pupil's interests, to arrange visits or extend contacts and provide further links to other associations. Research the history of the local regiment, hospital, football team, shopping centre or school.

Design questionnaires and collect information from local shopkeepers, priests, the police, bus drivers or pensioners. How do local shops cope with competition from multinationals? How are local bus routes and train services devised and do they meet everyone's needs. What provision exists in the area for mothers and young children: mother and toddler groups, library story times, child-friendly cafes, children's services at the local churches and health centre opening hours? Display interesting discoveries about local areas on a 'Did you know?' notice board.

*Six interesting historical facts about Chislehurst*

1   The name 'Chislehurst' is derived from the Saxon words 'cisel' meaning gravel and 'hyrst' meaning wooded hill.
2   Napoleon III was originally buried in St Mary's Church, Chislehurst.
3   Chislehurst Common was a popular Bank Holiday destination for Londoners in the early twentieth century.
4   During World War II, thousands of people used Chislehurst Caves as an air raid shelter.
5   Jimi Hendrix, the Who and the Rolling Stones all played in the Caves in the 1960s.
6   A water tower used to straddle the road from Chislehurst to Bromley. It was demolished in 1963 because its narrow archway meant that double-decker buses were unable to use the road.

Have fun and encourage appropriate daydreaming. When a sense of fun and pleasure in learning can be maintained, learning is less likely to be seen as a chore or threatening. Pupils will often have their best ideas when their brains are not bogged down with humdrum or concerned their answer might not be correct.

Talk to teachers of other subjects and draw the pupil's attention to cross-curricular links. Join with other departments to organise cross-curricular activities to help pupils see topics outside subject boxes and apply knowledge and understanding laterally.

It might be of interest to ask colleagues working in other departments how they would tackle specific pieces of work. They may approach a topic from a completely different angle that some pupils might appreciate for the novelty or change of focus.

## 2 Encourage pupils to ask questions

Ask questions and encourage pupils to ask questions. For less confident pupils, allow thirty seconds to discuss and check possible responses to the question with a neighbour. All questioning techniques have advantages and disadvantages. In a 'hands-up' approach, feedback will only be collected from pupils who process information quickly and accurately, although the teacher may assume these pupils' responses reflect the understanding of all. When pupils are allowed to discuss a question in pairs or small groups before responding, the teacher will have little idea of the content of the individual discussions. If there are teaching or support assistants working within the class, they can play an important monitoring role in such situations and provide feedback to the teacher about the level of understanding of different individuals.

Use open-ended and supplementary questions to extend pupils' curiosity. Use subject-specific vocabulary in order to familiarise pupils with the correct terminology, always ensuring the pupils understand the meanings of the words. Use higher-order questioning – as in Bloom's Taxonomy (1956) (see below). The idea being to move away from the questions that require the pupil to regurgitate the information (knowledge questions) towards more lateral, creative thinking (evaluation questions).

### Bloom's Taxonomy

1   *Knowledge.* Pupils show that they know and can recall knowledge. Knowledge questioning will use such words as define, label, list, recall and locate. 'List the types of soft engineering.' 'List the ways ...'
2   *Comprehension.* Pupils demonstrate understanding by explaining why something happened, and the similarities or the differences between situations. Comprehension questioning will use such

words as explain, contrast, name and illustrate. 'Explain how your model would work.' 'Contrast the behaviour of the village children with the behaviour of Amy in this scene.'

3 *Application.* Pupils use their knowledge to problem solve. Application questioning will use words such as solve, modify, summarise, predict and interpret. 'How could we modify Jamie's answer to make his point clearer?' 'Where else might this be useful?'

4 *Analysis.* Pupils are encouraged to see the overview and how new information fits into the whole. Analysis questioning will use such words as compare, relate, justify, contrast and categorise. 'What is the evidence for answer A?' 'How can Holly justify her point of view?'

5 *Synthesis.* Pupils are asked to use their knowledge in creative ways. Synthesis questioning will use such words as design, forecast, predict, discuss and invent. 'Could your group predict any changes that our third alternative would make? Discuss the positives and negatives.'

6 *Evaluation.* Pupils make decisions and judgements. Evaluation questioning will use such words as judge, evaluate, criticise and recommend. 'What would you judge to be the most significant arguments for and against?' 'What reasons would you give for making that specific prediction?'

### 3 Focus on the development of different types of thinking skills

Use different types of thinking skills to encourage a balance of creative and critical thinking. Use creative thinking to generate and extend ideas. This sort of thinking will build on previous suggestions and the production of as many varied and extreme ideas as possible. The focus of creative thinking is on the generation of ideas rather than their usefulness. It is divergent rather than deductive or analytical.

Critical thinking is the type of thinking that requires the individual to analyse and evaluate information, to seek alternatives and change opinions based on evidence and reasoning. The following types of information processing would be seen as critical thinking:

- Reasoning in order to draw inferences and make deductions.
- Information processing in order to sort, classify, compare and contrast.
- Evaluating in order to judge and develop criteria for assessing ideas.
- Enquiry in order to ask relevant questions, to plan, research and predict ideas.

## 4 Provide a supportive and inclusive environment

It is important to remember that an individual must have a degree of competency before they can be creative. As pupils become more experienced in their thinking, they will become increasingly adept at identifying good ideas but initially they will need to feel able to express novel or extreme ideas without fear of ridicule. Creativity will be limited if pupils are worried that they will get something wrong. They need to be reminded that it doesn't matter if their idea doesn't work as it may spark another idea that will. Even apparently obvious questions should be treated with respect as it can be hard to predict what the pupil has in mind.

Promote openness to experimentation and a willingness to take risks. Encourage pupils to step slightly outside their comfort zone and do something a little unusual. Suggest pupils explore new, maybe more extreme, ideas, explaining that the more ideas they try, the more theories they will be able to consider. Point out that most new ideas are combinations of old ideas that have been assembled or developed in a different way. New recipes are always based on old recipes: alternative ways to cook the dish, new ingredients that might be added or different sides that could be served with the meal.

Encourage discussion between pupils and teacher. Establish an atmosphere in the classroom that will help pupils communicate their ideas to others. Talking through different ideas can slow the pupils' work rate, allowing time to think around their plans, consult others and make their end product more considered.

Respect pupils' differences and learning preference. Many pupils prefer to work alone but, when they have the opportunity to work collaboratively with their peers, they will begin to appreciate their usefulness in opening up alternative avenues of thought. Give marks for originality in work and value humour and quirky ideas.

Display work in progress as well as the final product. Such displays will allow pupils to focus on the process as well as the end result and give time for reflection. Encourage pupils to plan their approach to a piece of work initially but then to take time out to reflect on their plan and change and adapt their approach. Include flexibility in all parts of the process.

Specialist Thinking Skills programmes, such as 'Philosophy for Children' (Lipman 1976), will provide ideas about initiating open-ended discussion in the classroom.

## 5  Maintain a flexible approach to learning

Devise long-term projects that run alongside class work to help pupils to see what it is like to be involved in ongoing activity and how the various stages in a process can be adapted and changed before they come together to make a whole.

Encourage flexible and individual thinking that recognises the originality of pupils' work. If teachers insist that students restrict themselves to thinking only about they know, their willingness to experiment will be reduced.

Focus on the application rather than recall of knowledge. Do not put an emphasis on conformity or neat presentation over creative thought. Involve pupils in lesson planning. Use pupil feedback. Which topics did they find challenging, interesting, boring or confusing? Which lessons did they particularly enjoy or find useful and why? What topic would they like to take further? Which topics did they find easy and which ones difficult? This sort of feedback will give teaching staff valuable information to use in order to adapt their teaching style and match their approach more closely to pupil need and preference.

## 6  Use a variety of teaching methods

Set work that provides a balance between challenge and achievement to give a combination of reassurance, yet allow for a testing of skill. Pupils' motivation will be increased when they feel teachers have high expectations of them.

Introduce the pupils to different methods of working to relieve boredom and increase motivation. Step away from routine and teach one lesson in a different way each week to avoid being predictable.

Use a multi-sensory input in order to accommodate different learning styles. Ask pupils to choose how they would like to present a piece of work: a group presentation, an individual project, a mind map, a comic strip sequence, a PowerPoint presentation, a whole-class question and answer session or role play. Accommodating different learning styles in lessons does not require a rigid adherence to differentiating for the visual, auditory and kinaesthetic learner as pupils' preferences will change depending on how they are feeling, what subject is being covered and what time of day it is.

Use experts, perhaps other members of staff, teachers from other schools, parents, older pupils or speakers from national or voluntary associations to give demonstrations or lectures. Pupils will respect adults with a good subject knowledge and enthusiasm for their specialist subject. Run options or workshops on vocational courses or as an introduction to slightly unusual hobbies: bell ringing, beauty therapy, patchwork and appliqué, writing fiction, go-karting, parkour, Russian or music mixing. Such input should be provided as part of the normal school day and not as an add-on. Add-ons will extend the working day for adult and child and may be perceived as unimportant, a child-minding provision or a public relations exercise.

Use IT. Set up links with other schools to enable pupils to work collaboratively. Using video conferencing and computer simulations, iPads and apps can provide an alternative way for pupils to engage with others.

Work on open-ended tasks with no correct answer. Some pupils like to be told the 'right' way to tackle activities, so encourage them to be happy with ambiguity. Give answers and ask the pupils to write the questions.

Create displays to showcase innovative pupil work or to demonstrate progress in a specific area, perhaps the development of the mobile phone, computer software or a particular area of medicine during the past twenty years.

## 7 Include problem solving, case studies and enquiry tasks in lessons

Pupils need to see problems and adversity as challenges. Giving pupils experience of problem solving will encourage them to take a similar attitude to the difficulties they face in life. 'How am I going to tackle this?' 'What can I do to improve the situation?' 'What sort of thing have I done before that might help here?' 'Who can I ask to help me get around this problem?'

Teach problem-solving techniques. There are numerous stand-alone problem-solving programmes, such as Edward de Bono's *Six Thinking Hats* (1985), that can provide an easily understood starting point.

Make problems relevant to real life. A lot of learning in the real world is practical: how to drive, how to swim, how to train a dog, how to cook, how to paint a room, how to buy a flat, how to mend a puncture, how to iron a shirt, how to assemble a wardrobe or how to play golf.

Help pupils to become experts in their areas of interest, to connect random ideas and use these for problem solving. They should look at problems from a number of viewpoints and use information from a range of sources, for example knowledge acquired from playing football to solve a problem in geography, or an understanding of how a bicycle works to solve a problem in science. Pupils should feel free to borrow other people's ideas, to adapt, refine and build on them.

Problem solving can provide an incentive for study and make a mundane topic seem interesting. Good problems will interest the pupil and capture their imagination, give opportunity for early success, but also have scope to extend and challenge, allow for a range of approaches and require solutions that need an understanding of a process and not merely the routine of following a process.

Show creativity and innovation in curriculum provision. Hold events during the year in which different school years, classes or individual pupils are taken off timetable to participate in introductory or taster courses, to have lectures from external speakers, to use specialist facilities at other schools or visit local museums, universities and colleges. Such events will provide staff and pupils with alternative ways of looking at teaching and learning.

Accept that pupils' reactions to some input within school is impossible to measure, that consequences may not be seen for five, ten or twenty years and feedback is unlikely to be received.

Do not be afraid to try teaching approaches that the school would not usually consider. Adults need to demonstrate courage and creativity rather than just pay lip service to ideals. Trial programmes that focus on the development of pupils' emotional needs, for example Circles for Learning (www.circlesforlearning.co.uk). Circles for Learning involves a monthly practical session over one calendar year, in which groups of children observe the interaction between a parent and baby, witnessing the month-on-month development of the infant's emotional responses, physical skills and social and linguistic ability. The programme focuses on the importance of the parent/child bond for the development of the babies' emotional well-being and so has relevance for pupils' future parenting skills.

Metacognition, social skills, self-confidence and creativity, as discussed in previous chapters, could be supported by alternative input involving incidental, as opposed to direct and structured learning. When pupils participate, for example, in sporting activities, enjoy adequate opportunities for free play or read for pleasure, they will be acquiring the competencies that underpin happiness and emotional well-being in a relaxed and sociable way.

Chapters 7, 8 and 9 discuss how schools could develop such incidental learning that benefits pupils' well-being without any need for direct adult intervention.

# References

Bloom, B. (1956) *Taxonomy of Educational Objectives.* Boston, MA: Allyn and Bacon (revised edition 1984 by Pearson Education).

de Bono, E. (1985) *Six Thinking Hats: An essential approach to business management.* Boston, MA: Little, Brown and Company.

Lipman, M. (1976) *Philosophy for Children.* Oxford: Basil Blackwell.

# Learning rather than teaching

## Three possible solutions

An alternative approach to developing well-being in children and young people would be to increase existing opportunities that do not require direct adult intervention but focus rather on the child *learning* incidentally. The advantages of such an approach would include: the pace of learning suiting the individual; the child taking pleasure in the experience; and the avoidance of unnecessary pressure or stress. Three examples of such approaches would be:

Solution 1: increased involvement in *sport*.

Solution 2: providing adequate opportunity to *play*.

Solution 3: promoting *reading* for pleasure.

# CHAPTER 7

# Solution 1
## Increased involvement in sport

Sport develops all of the attributes that are necessary for mental and physical well-being, and yet the benefits of PE and Games for children and young people are often overlooked by educational authorities, with physical activity sidelined as an optional extra in the curriculum. The number of children participating in sport has declined over recent years. In 2006, 70 per cent of boys and 59 per cent of girls were meeting daily recommended activity levels. In 2008, 28 per cent of thirteen-to-fifteen-year-old boys were taking the recommended amount of exercise. By 2012, when the Olympics took place in London, this number had halved to 14 per cent. For girls over the same period, the figure fell from 14 per cent to 8 per cent (Health and Social Care Information Centre 2015).

Over 10,000 school playing fields were sold off between 1980 and 2010, the equivalent of approximately one playing field each day. In 2011, Michael Gove, the then Education Secretary, cut the £162 million that had been ring-fenced to develop school sport through the SSP (School Sport Partnerships). SSP funding was replaced by PE and sport premiums. Primary schools received £9,000 a year to spend on the delivery of PE, while secondary schools received no PE and sport premium funding.

The development of sport within schools does not require government appointed Sports Tsars, sporting role models presenting prizes at Speech Days or the use of independent schools' playing fields during the summer holidays. The true integration of sport into children's lives is about giving all children from nursery through to sixth-form the chance to exercise on a regular basis. When opportunities for PE,

Dance, Games and Sport are part of every school day, all children can take pleasure in physical activity from an early age and grow up seeing exercise as a normal part of everyday life.

Activities do not need to be challenging, complicated or follow specialist programmes with levels to be achieved and targets met. Physical activity in childhood is just play, good fun and a natural part of growing up. When children and young people assume it is normal to cycle or walk to school, climb trees, go swimming, walk the dog, bike to the shops, play active games in the school playground and roller-skate or skateboard in the park, they are more likely to incorporate exercise into their daily routine and less likely to be at risk from obesity, diabetes or poor general health. The more children and young people are involved in sport, the more confident they will become in their physical ability, increasing the likelihood of further activity, which in turn will improve their performance and establish a positive cycle of participation.

Games for younger children do not need a trained coach, equipment or specialist clothing. When children only attend structured sport lessons, they may find it harder to devise their own variations of games or to feel free to adapt rules to their particular circumstances. Cricket does not need a team of eleven, a particular size and type of bat and ball or to have twenty metres between each set of stumps. Four children can play 'cricket' with a tennis racket and ball, a box for stumps and run up and down the garden once to score a run. In the same way that an individual does not need specialist training or equipment to read, to sing, to glue a model or to paint pictures with a young child, playing games and becoming involved in simple physical activity is within every adult's capability. Adults who the children see as non-specialists are more likely to enthuse pupils. They will not be seen as experts far removed from the child's own levels of fitness and competence, but as enthusiastic amateurs.

Activities that could be easily organised in school include:

1 Orienteering courses set up around the school grounds.
2 Liaison with other schools for joint sport taster days. Share any specialist facilities or input from enthusiasts in the schools.

3 Ask parents to introduce and demonstrate the sports they enjoy. Show videos of different kinds of sports.

4 A loan system that enables pupils to borrow equipment from school and sales of any old, but serviceable, PE stock.

5 Opportunities to try out different kinds of dance: disco, tap, street dancing, salsa, country dancing, swing, line dancing, hip hop or the use of dance mats.

6 Promoting variations of indoor games: five-a-side hockey, football rounders, French cricket, Korfball and walking football.

7 The use of a variety of playground equipment to practise basic skills: Velcro glove and ball sets, juggling balls, boom bats, badminton sets, stilts or foot pots. Hopscotch grids, hoopla, skittles or hoops. Frisbee throwing and catching games. Boules. Skipping and French skipping.

8 Encouraging lunchtime supervisors to organise physically active games: Hide and Seek, Chase, It, Grandma's Footsteps, Piggy in the Middle, What's the Time Mr Wolf?, Mr Crocodile and Follow the Leader.

9 Training circuits set up in the playground: ten star jumps followed by twenty skips, five runs across the playground and ten press-ups.

10 Teaching children traditional songs and games that involve physical movement: Oranges and Lemons, Simon Says, The Farmer's in his Den, I Sent a Letter to my Love, In and Out the Dusty Bluebells and Heads, Shoulders, Knees and Toes.

## What can sport do to promote well-being?

### 1 Demonstrate the advantages of collaboration and teamwork

Players in any team will need to listen to the advice of others, they will be free to express their own opinions, but teams will need to work together to improve overall team performance. The team is always more important than the individual. A player may prefer to play on the wing but, if the team manager feels she contributes more by playing in a central position, then that is where she will be expected to play. Players may be left on the bench for half a match if their fitness is in question or they do not fit a game plan, yet each player will be expected to give of their best in every game and not let their team down. They must support the team whoever is playing and no matter how they feel personally. This will give a valuable lesson in humility. In return, all players will be supported by the other members of their team, as everyone will know how it feels to be left out of a side, be substituted, injured or have a poor game.

## 2  Develop 'good sportsmanship'

Sport develops self-discipline and self-control, in other words 'good sportsmanship'. Players are expected to behave in the correct way; if they break the rules, they will be sent off the field and disadvantage their team. Break the rules in life and you will let down your friends and family. Sport teaches the individual to take responsibility for their own behaviour. All players will want to win, but they must learn how to win or lose with good grace. The player may realise that an umpire has made a poor decision, but they must accept this as part of the game: sometimes life is unfair.

> We hold up our sport and praise it for the way referees conduct themselves and how players conduct themselves with referees.
>
> (Lawrence Dallaglio, former captain of the England Rugby team)

Many young children will cheat, sulk or walk away if they lose a game. Participation in sport will help pupils to develop control of their emotions. Pupils who play sport will realise that the way they behave towards others may be a reflection of their own feelings of anger, jealously, disappointment or frustration and little to do with the other person. This can give valuable insights into the behaviour of others. When a friend makes fun of them and they know that they have done nothing wrong, the pupil will realise that the problem is more to do with the friend's own worries or insecurities.

## 3 Develop motivation

Choice will always improve an individual's motivation. Sport offers pupils a choice from a huge diversity of activities: cross-country running, badminton, hang gliding, triathlon, rowing, horse riding, volleyball, weightlifting, trampolining, aerobics, bowls, mountaineering, judo, swimming, boxing, snooker, tennis, ice hockey, athletics, cycling, lacrosse or keep-fit. All pupils will be able to find a sport they can enjoy. There are sporting activities for individuals and pairs, as well as for large and small teams. Yoga, martial arts, fitness training, table tennis, rounders, golf, as well as the traditional team games of netball, hockey, football, cricket and rugby.

Being part of a team will increase motivation. The player might not feel like turning out on a wet afternoon in November, but will do so because they cannot let down their team.

Sport can motivate individuals by giving them a reason to exercise. Many people will participate in fun runs, long-distance bike rides, skip-a-thons, table tennis or dancing marathons for charity, being happy to exercise and raise money for a good cause.

Anyone involved in sport will have been motivated to achieve specific targets: to run a marathon, increase their level of fitness, enjoy the company of like-minded people, produce a better time or distance, get into a team, play regularly for a team, or move up from the second team to the first team. They will have planned how to reach their target, perhaps by changing their training schedule, becoming a member of a different club, changing position in a team or using new equipment. They set themselves aims and then devise a small-step approach towards achieving those aims. This gives an individual valuable experience in long-term planning in everyday life, breaking challenges down into a small steps and appreciating that persistence and hard work will pay off eventually.

## 4 Develop self-discipline and delayed gratification

Sport places emphasis on training the mind as well as the body. Through involvement in sport, pupils will learn how to listen carefully, how to follow instructions, to develop self-control, self-discipline, concentration and personal organisation. Players face mental as well as physical challenges and will be presented with opportunities to demonstrate their mental fitness alongside their physical strength. A lot of training in sport relates to mental attitude and how players can channel their nervous energy into their performance.

> People can put as much expectation on our shoulders as they want. It's down to us to block that out and concentrate on our performance.
>
> (Joanna Rowsell, British track cycling team)

When players are not selected for teams, they do not sulk or give up as they know that would not be a solution, they simply work harder. They improve their performance by *doing* something; they do not read a book about gymnastics or listen to a talk about speed skating, they go out and improve their training, practising harder or more effectively.

Training must be carried out regularly whether or not the individual is in the mood and sacrifices made for long-term benefits. Olympic champions or international players can seem to appear from nowhere, but this is never the case; each player will have been training and competing for years.

> You compete against a vast array of people and train your whole life for these moments. When it finally clicked at the London Olympics, it was after seven years as a pro.
>
> (Greg Rutherford, Gold Medallist, London Olympics 2012)

Athletes take a long-term view to their sport, understanding that there is no such thing as a quick fix. This is a good lesson for life: very few people are successful overnight, however it may appear to the casual observer. Success in a sport always requires delayed gratification.

> You have to keep working, you cannot afford to be lazy at any stage, you will be found out.
>
> (Andy Gomarsall, professional Rugby Union player)

## 5  Encourage individuals to be courageous and try new things

The fear of looking silly can stop pupils from doing anything new, but trying different approaches and learning from errors teaches athletes valuable lessons. Experimenting will show up weaknesses and help find better ways of working. Dick Fosbury, an American high jumper, first started experimenting with new high jump techniques at the age of sixteen while still at school. Fosbury was experiencing problems using the dominant jumping techniques of the time and so practised alternatives including a 'flop' jump that meant he crossed the bar on his back rather than front. Although he faced early scepticism, Fosbury persevered and achieved success, winning a gold medal in the high jump in the 1968 Olympics. The 'Fosbury Flop' is now the jumping technique used by all serious high jumpers.

## 6  Develop self-esteem

Spending free time involved in sporting activity has been shown to reduce the amount of time children and teenagers spend online. Young people whose social lives revolve around Facebook and social media sites are more likely to worry about the opinions of others than those teenagers who have real-life contacts and hobbies. When using Facebook, it would be easy to imagine that everyone else is popular, has more material possessions, leads exciting and meaningful lives and that your own life compares unfavourably. British psychologist Oliver James believes that placing value on possessions and appearance in this way increases the risk of mental disorders, and that this can be particularly relevant for girls. However, when girls mix in the real world with other females with similar interests and are surrounded by others who behave in the same way, there will be no need for them to pretend they are something they're not. They will be less likely to conform to female stereotyping and worry about their appearance, popularity or body shape.

'I'm slim because I can't carry excess weight in long-distance races.' 'Being tall is a fantastic advantage for an attacking player.' 'I'm wearing jogging bottoms because I'm on my way to the gym.' 'Being petite is essential for my agility.' 'I can't grow my finger nails long because of netball rules.' 'I have broad shoulders because I swim for the county.'

Boys who are members of mixed swimming, rowing and football clubs will take it for granted that female club members will be powerfully built, have calloused hands or be covered in bruises.

> I love my big thighs; I wouldn't be able to pick up a hammer without them. I put blood, sweat and tears into building them up.
>
> (Sophie Hitchon, British record holder for hammer throwing)

## 7 Give experience of dealing with failure

Life is competitive and sport gives children experience of coping with failure in manageable doses: losing a running race in the garden with siblings, losing a school hockey match or an inter-class tennis match. Resilience is essential at all levels of sport. The pupil might not make the school's 'U14' team or fail to be selected for a club squad, but they will know there is no point in giving up; they must merely increase their effort. Anyone who is involved in sport has an immediate advantage in terms of resilience. They are certain to have dealt with disappointment whatever their standard of play. Players will see failure as an essential part of progress, will understand that they will have another opportunity to prove themselves and use that knowledge to motivate themselves: there will be another match next week, training tomorrow, the tournament next month or next year's final. I will be there and get my revenge/prove I can do it/give my best performance ever.

Michael Phelps, an American swimmer who won a total of twenty-two medals (including eighteen gold medals) in three Olympic Games, was motivated by his failure in his first Olympics in Sydney when he was fifteen. 'Going there, fit and losing. That really hurt.'

> I have missed more than 9,000 shots in my career. I have lost almost 300 games. On twenty-six occasions I have been entrusted to take the game winning shot, and I missed. I have failed over and over and over again in my life. And that is why I succeed.
>
> (Michael Jordan, US basketball player)

In 1998, footballer David Beckham was sent off in the World Cup second-round match against Argentina for a retaliatory kick against an Argentinean player. England went on to lose on penalties with disappointed fans holding Beckham responsible for the defeat. Beckham's humiliation could not have been more public. However, his continued commitment to the game and his determination to learn from such mistakes were rewarded when he captained England for the first time two years later in 2000.

See Section IV, 'Resilience: developing pupils' resilience'.

## 8 Give opportunities to extend friendship groups

Sports clubs offer the perfect environment for establishing friendships with others who have similar interests. Anyone involved in sport outside school will have different sets of friends and different skills that enable them to feel good about themselves. Friendships out of school help pupils to keep a social balance and not become over-dependent on one group of peers. Pupils will know older players, younger players, players from other teams, coaches, referees and team captains. Connecting with adults who are interested and supportive can make a difference to pupils' self-esteem. Coaches, club and team captains will not be interested in the child's performance in the classroom but see their sporting potential. Schools can help by establishing links with local clubs, sports centres and fitness studios as well as national associations to enable pupils to access facilities outside their local area: mountaineering, sailing, canoeing, skiing, surfing or potholing clubs, or create links with specialist facilities that the school does not have space to provide: archery ranges, cycle tracks, horse-riding centres or golf ranges.

Having friends and teammates from different age ranges and sectors of the community will increase pupils' confidence when they socialise in the future. Joining a sports club will provide an immediate social network when pupils leave school, move to a new town, start a new job or go to college or university. They will not be going to a car maintenance or embroidery evening class to try to make friends but joining a badminton, rugby or hockey club to play badminton, rugby or hockey and will make friends with other players incidentally.

Sport centres provide places for teenagers to socialise. Teenagers can go to the local ice rink, swimming pool, bowling alley, skate board park with no need for ice skating, swimming, bowling or skate boarding lessons or being able to perform to a high level, they can just go to have fun and meet their peers.

## 9 Promote a healthy lifestyle

When pupils are interested in sport, they will also be interested in health and fitness and be more knowledgeable about what constitutes a good diet, and the dangers of smoking, excessive drinking and a sedentary lifestyle. When teenagers are members of sports clubs, they will be surrounded by role models who take their health and fitness seriously. It is easier to resist peer pressure if you can say that you are not smoking or drinking at the moment because you are training for an important match. Such an excuse may be more acceptable to peers than a simple refusal.

The role that sleep plays in maintaining physical health is becoming increasingly apparent. All athletes will know the value of taking adequate rest and participating in sport, particularly when outdoors, will lead to physical tiredness as opposed to mental exhaustion. Physical tiredness is more likely to result in deeper and longer sleep. Research shows the link between sleep and brain function. According to Wagner *et al.* (2004): 'Regular and sufficient sleep is essential for the brain to learn effectively.'

The long-term physical benefits of sport are well documented. Exercise has been shown to reduce the risk of dementia, sharpen memory and release endorphins which improve the participant's mood, as well as suppressing the release of stress hormones. Participation in sport will make pupils feel good. Athletes will take pleasure from being fit and in good shape.

> I've got the tone of a swimmer, the leanness of a runner, strong thighs from riding and good glutes from fencing.
>
> (Samantha Murray, Olympic Silver Medallist, modern pentathlete)

A Public Health England study (2014) showed that whole-school approaches to health and well-being were linked to an increase in pupils' readiness and willingness to learn. For advice relating to a healthy lifestyle, see Section IV, pupil advice sheet: 'A healthy lifestyle'.

## 10  Promote inclusive approaches

Every local authority will organise sports classes for all levels of ability, gender and age: Baby Gym, Golf for Beginners, Return to Netball, Advanced Squash, Football for Girls, Adult Non-swimmers, Mother and Baby Aerobics, Badminton Improvers, Riding for the Visually Impaired or Walking Football for the Retired. Numerous individual associations and clubs will organise free taster events with an emphasis on inclusivity, sociability and enjoyment.

> Parkrun organise free, weekly, 5km timed runs around the world. They are open to everyone, free, safe and easy to take part in. These events take place in pleasant parkland surroundings and we encourage people of every ability to take part; from those taking their first steps in running to Olympians; from juniors to those with more experience.
>
> (www.parkrun.org.uk)

Everyone can participate in some form of sport, no matter their age, level of ability, disability, level of fitness, social group or gender. When a pupil claims not to enjoy sport, they mean they have not found the sport they enjoy yet. To raise pupil awareness of the range of opportunities open to them, school social events and trips could involve visits to sporting venues: bowling alleys, climbing and diving centres, go-kart tracks, archery ranges, ski domes, equestrian centres, ice-skating rinks or golf ranges. Early exposure to a variety of different sports can create satisfying, lifelong hobbies.

While there will be some sort of sport for everyone to enjoy, children with specific learning difficulties may enjoy specific types of physical activity. Pupils with Asperger's syndrome may prefer individual sports such as mountaineering, orienteering or long-distance running. Pupils with ADHD will benefit from the development of self-control and focus required by martial arts. Pupils with dyspraxia will benefit from sports that encourage the development of core muscles and stability, such as trampolining or horse riding.

Clubs are welcoming to individuals who want to be involved in a non-participatory capacity: coaches, track officials, umpires; scorers, caddies, referees, team managers or linesmen. Being a fan of a club brings instant membership of a large and local social group with shared uniform, knowledge of the sport and topics of conversation.

Sport is easy to organise and can be carried out individually with no need for other players (jogging, yoga, swimming, keep-fit, skipping) or in pairs and small groups (badminton, squash, tennis) or as part of a team (netball, hockey, bowls, rugby, football). Pupils can work out in the home, garden or park with no specialist equipment required. Some adults will find it motivating to have a personal trainer, wear designer sportswear or have a cross-trainer in the living room, but none of this is necessary. If an individual feels the need to exercise, they can run up and down the stairs or put on trainers and run around the block.

## 11  Provide different levels of challenge

The individual can chose their level of challenge within a sport. Sport can be high physical risk: mountaineering, skydiving, potholing, parkour; or low physical risk: snooker, darts or table tennis. Some pupils will enjoy extreme sports and overcoming fear, while participating in such sports will increase their self-confidence in other situations. Other individuals will gain a sense of achievement from diving off the side of a swimming pool for fifty years without feeling any need to progress to higher boards or introduce turns, twists or somersaults to their dives. As long as they are confident enough in the water to enjoy swimming with their family while on holiday, they will feel their level of skill is sufficient. Children can go horse riding for years and simply enjoy riding the horse around a field without having any desire to learn to canter, gallop or jump. In a marathon, runners may participate to secure a good position in the rankings, run to improve a previous time, run to support a friend, run to raise money for a favourite charity or run simply to try to complete the course.

> **Key point**
>
> There is no need to progress in a sport; it can be undertaken purely for pleasure.

The degree of challenge is chosen by the individual. Athletes select their level of stress; some will interpret what others might see as pressure to be excitement and challenge. Stress can be viewed in positive ways. This is a valuable lesson for life: if an individual can view adversity as a challenge, they will be able to employ strategies to tackle and resolve difficult situations in everyday life.

## 12 Provide opportunities to use and appreciate different types of intelligence

The different intelligences that are used in sport allow different groups of individuals to realise success. 'The reason a football player is described as a genius when he is clearly no Einstein is because he has phenomenal technical skill' (Campbell 2015).

> Dance is more than a hobby. It's as important as anything else on the curriculum. It's as important as Maths, it's as important as being a doctor.
>
> (Akram Khan, choreographer)

Sport can be kinaesthetically beautiful with grace seen in physical movement: the precision of a high board dive, a goal scored from an impossible angle, a perfect performance in a gym routine, or a smooth, successful set piece in netball.

Sport gives many pupils a reason to go to school. They may not belong to traditionally academic groups, but the kudos gained through their involvement in sport enables them to feel part of, and identify with, the school. Success in sport can make all the difference to a pupil's self-esteem.

> I struggled academically because I suffer from dyslexia. Sport was always the escape route. Having a ball in my hand was the best thing that could happen to let me express myself.
>
> (Ben Youngs, national rugby player)

## 13 Provide release from stress

The hormones that are released when an individual feels anxious are burnt off during physical activity and do not remain in the body manifesting themselves in symptoms such as headaches, stomach aches and general malaise. When stress is an ongoing issue for pupils, they may turn to unhealthy behaviours, perhaps smoking or using alcohol or drugs to cope with their feelings, but when a physically active teenager feels under pressure because of exams or an excessive workload, they know they will feel better after going for a run, a bike ride or a swim.

Playing sport is a perfect way to reduce anxiety. If pupils go out with friends to watch a film, go for a meal or watch television, they will still be able to focus on their worries, but if they are playing in a rugby, netball, squash, tennis or five-a-side football match, they cannot afford to think about anything else, they will have to concentrate on the game and enjoy a respite from worrying thoughts.

Sport can provide individuals with an opportunity to re-focus and be at one with nature. Experiencing affinity with the natural world can help pupils to relax, slow down, helping them to see beauty in their surroundings and putting their worries into perspective.

> It's a beautiful thing, to go deeper and deeper, and eventually stop swimming and just drop into the deep blue.
>
> (Ben Noble, founder of the Australian Free Diving Association)

## 14 Present real-life moral and social issues for discussion

Social and moral questions can be highlighted using sporting issues as a basis for discussion: the use of performance-enhancing drugs, the control of clubs by corporate businesses, animal rights in horse racing, opportunities for the disabled, and racial and gender inequality.

UNICEF has joined with the Malawi national netball squad to promote women's education and health in Africa.

> We are working together to promote national campaigns to reduce violence against women and girls and improve girls' chances of finishing

school and delaying marriage. Through this ground breaking partnership, girls across Malawi will be supported to grow up healthy, safe and well educated.

(Liz Twyford, UNICEF)

Sport presents children with relaxing ways to develop strength of character, self-control and levels of physical fitness, all vital factors in the maintenance of happiness throughout life. A second way to enable pupils to maintain mental and physical health would be to provide generous opportunities for free play. This will be discussed in Chapter 8.

## References

Campbell, A. (2015) *Winners: And how they succeed.* London: Hutchinson.

Health and Social Care Information Centre (2015) *Health and Wellbeing of Fifteen Year Olds in England.* Leeds.

Public Health England (2014) *The Link Between Pupil Health and Wellbeing and Attainment: A briefing for head teachers, governors and staff in education settings.* London: Department of Health.

Wagner, U., Gais, S., Haider, H., Verleger, R and Born, J. (2004) Sleep inspires insight. *Nature*, 427: 352–5.

# CHAPTER 8

# Solution 2

## Providing adequate opportunity for play

## All children need to have adequate opportunity to play

'Play is an essential part of every child's life and is vital for the enjoyment of childhood as well as social, emotional, intellectual and physical development' (www.playengland.org). Play contributes to children's cognitive, physical, social and emotional development, and is so important for children's well-being that it has been recognised by the United Nations High Commission for Human Rights as a right of every child. The right to play and enjoy informal recreation, for all children and young people up to eighteen years of age, is contained in Article 31 of the UN Convention on the Rights of the Child. Despite the recognition of the benefits of play, there has been a significant reduction in the amount of free time available for children to play during the past thirty years.

### Why is play important for children's physical and mental well-being?

#### 1 Play develops children's physical skills

Play develops children's physical ability: their strength, stamina, spatial awareness and hand–eye coordination. Any relaxation time that involves physical activity will enable the children to develop these skills in a natural and enjoyable way.

Pupils burn off surplus energy through movement and an hour of active, undirected play during the day will increase focus and attention in the classroom. When young children begin to fidget and lose concentration, a short break in which they can move about will help them to re-focus and settle. Morning and afternoon playtimes offer perfect re-energising activity.

## 2 Play helps in the development of pupils' social skills

Free play allows children to work in groups, to share, develop empathy, negotiate, listen to others, learn conflict resolution techniques, acquire an understanding of body language and develop self-advocacy. Children's language will develop at a 'needs must' level. They will want to communicate with peers, so will be motivated to experiment with new words, use longer sentences and speak more clearly to make themselves understood and enrich their play experience.

## 3 Play helps to build strong bonds between parents and children

When parents observe or join their children in play activities, they are given an insight into their children's world. By listening to their children as they play, parents may be alerted to any concerns and worries and be able to intervene to clarify confusions or offer reassurance.

Some of the best parent/child interactions occur during periods of relaxation at home, when parents are playing games in the home or garden, chatting with the children, gardening or visiting friends.

## 4 Play is fun for children

Play is fun, a natural way to learn and gives children time to relax and to think. Play cannot be replaced by formal teaching. Many skills can only be acquired through repeated physical activity: a child will learn to walk, hop, jump or climb by walking, hopping, jumping or climbing. When children are enjoying themselves and the activity is fun, they will put in the required practice without thought. When young children play with a ball, they will develop the skills necessary to play cricket, netball or football. When children play on sit-and-ride toys and scooters, they will develop the balance necessary to ride a bike. If children are 'taught' to ride a bike, they will not have the same level of motivation as when playing on a bike. In play, the child can scoot along without using the pedals, ride the bike for five minutes and then get off to do something else, cycle on grass or on a tarmac path, ride up and down an incline, bounce down a step or cycle round in a circle for half an hour as part of some other game. They will learn new skills incidentally as they play.

Free play enables children to be absorbed in their own interests for long periods of time, reducing feelings of stress and ensuring that they are happy, engaged and motivated.

### 5 Make-believe play

Play allows children to learn about themselves and others. Make-believe play offers children the chance to act out aspects of their own lives that may be puzzling or frightening, to deal with difficult situations and see how it might feel to be somebody else. The children can create a world they can master, helping them to conquer their fears and try out ideas. When playing hospitals, schools or dentists, they can put themselves in situations they can withdraw from whenever necessary. The dentist can look at their teeth and say that everything is fine, that they are too young to visit the dentist and they will mend their mother's teeth instead or wave a fairy wand and make everyone's teeth perfect. Everything is under the child's control.

### 6 Pre-school learning

It has been shown that play helps children adjust to the school setting and enhances their learning readiness, learning behaviours and problem-solving skills. Play in early years establishes the foundations for later learning. Missing out on early play experiences will leave gaps in children's understanding. When children paint, colour or play with Lego, beads or plasticine, they are acquiring the fine motor skills necessary for writing. When pupils play with sand and water, they are developing an understanding of the properties of solids and liquids. When understanding is born of practical experience, children are less likely to make apparently bizarre errors during later school years. Riding a scooter will teach about speed and centres of gravity, roller-skating about friction and surfaces, throwing a ball about velocity and angles. Such life experience cannot be taught through a formal teaching approach. Many parents feel that computer programmes aid their children's learning, but it is essential that children's early learning is practical and based in the real, rather than the virtual, world.

### 7 Fosters a spirit of the local community

Providing space for children to play locally will promote community spirit within the neighbourhood with facilities used by children for play becoming a focal point for other groups: sports teams, teenagers, pensioners, joggers and dog walkers. Easily accessible, outdoor community spaces have an important role in the everyday lives of the local community and provide a safe venue for all ages to meet and socialise.

### 8 Develops creative thought

Play fosters the flexibility of thought required by society for future progress. Providing children with greater opportunities for free play will make them more creative thinkers. The academic pressures of the school curriculum are eroding the study of the creative arts in school in addition to reducing opportunities for play. There is a danger of a decline in the ability of young people to be creative and able to generate the new ideas essential for the progress and development of society.

## Why have opportunities for play been reduced?

Despite the numerous benefits known to derive from play, time for free play has been markedly reduced over the past forty years. Long-term studies of children's play in the US found that, not only did children play less, but they also had less time for free, non-directed play with more activities being imposed on them.

A poll commissioned by Play England in 2007 found that 71 per cent of adults played out on their street every day during childhood compared with only 21 per cent of children in 2007. There are many explanations for the current trends, but several key factors need to be considered:

1   The changes in attitude towards parenting that have led to 'professional parenting'.
2   The pressure felt by schools to focus on academic achievement.
3   The reduction in family free time as a result of an increase in the number of working parents.
4   The influence of TV and multimedia.
5   The development of commercialism in all areas of children's lives.

## 1 Professional parents

Many parents work in high-pressure environments where they are judged by their productivity and requiring 'down time' is seen as a weakness; every moment must be maximised and used effectively. 'Professional' parents may approach childrearing in the same way. When they are aware of any shortcomings in their child's skills, they will put compensatory tactics into place, in the same way they would offer support to a work colleague who was falling behind. Time is tight, so the desired skill must be acquired as quickly as possible by, for example, the children going to swimming lessons rather than being taken to the pool at weekends to play in the water. Playing is fun, occurs at the individual child's pace and is a pleasurable way to relax. When the child learns to swim through play, swimming will be a pleasurable activity and one they will continue to enjoy in the future. The child will be able to relish jumping into the pool, going down a slide, swimming under the water or splashing a parent or sibling, with skills acquired as a by-product. The professional parent may see play as wasting time: the child needs to learn to swim quickly and properly. Lessons will not teach doggy paddle, but the correct technique for front crawl. Learning correct swimming strokes would be better taught after the basics of water confidence have been acquired. Very few individuals become Olympic swimmers, but many will enjoy time at the swimming pool or in the sea while on holiday.

Professional parents will want to maximise their assets and so their children will need to develop into multi-talented individuals. The children will be given a wealth of additional opportunities to give them an edge over their peers, taking music, ballet, sport, drama and language lessons from a very early age. Children will be encouraged to build their CV through both academic excellence and participation in an extensive variety of extra-curricular activities. Encouraging children to view all activities in terms of 'Would this look good on my UCAS personal statement?' will reduce the likelihood of children doing anything purely for pleasure. Professional parents are likely to listen to the chatter of their colleagues and become frightened by how busy other children's lives appear to be and the sacrifices other parents appear to be making. Pupils' after-school hours will be filled with additional tutoring, music lessons and extra-curricular clubs, reducing the time for relaxation and the type of imaginative and physical play necessary for the development of creativity, social cooperation and the promotion of mental health. Children do not develop into well-rounded, socially competent individuals through hot housing.

## 2  Academic pressure within schools

In response to an increase in testing in schools, many children are forced into rigorous academic schedules from a very early age. The curriculum time allowed for creative subjects in school and children's play time has been cut to allow extra focus on those academic subjects that will be tested and used to measure the school's performance. Breakfast clubs and after-school childcare will focus on more of the same academic activity and extra homework provided rather than time allowed for relaxation, free play and physical activity. It is unnecessary for children in KS1 to be given homework and children in KS2 have far better things to do with their free time.

## 3 Working parents

As a result of an increase in the number of working parents, fewer families can care for their children in their own homes during the day, making it necessary for children to be in nurseries, pre-school provision and before and after school care. When the children get home, they will be too tired to play.

## 4 The influence of TV and multimedia

In some communities, children cannot play safely outside the home unless they are supervised by adults, so they have to be entertained inside for significant periods of time with television, computer or video games. Parents will use the television, computer or multimedia gadgets to amuse their children safely and quietly within the home. According to Baroness Greenfield, Senior Research Fellow at Lincoln College, Oxford University (2011), the average child will spend almost 2,000 hours in front of a screen between their tenth and eleventh birthdays.

## 5 Commercialism

Parents are under pressure from magazines, the internet and commercial companies suggesting that there are more valuable means of promoting success and happiness in children than the tried and trusted methods of play and family togetherness. Specialised gyms and enrichment courses designed for children exist in most communities and there is an abundance of additional commercial after-school activities. Such courses are heavily promoted and many parents are persuaded that they are essential for the children's development. Once one child begins to attend such a programme, other parents may worry that their child will be left behind and companies are able to feed off parental anxiety. An inordinate amount of potential parent–child relaxation time will be spent transporting tired children between such activities as they will run after school, at weekends or during the holidays when children should be enjoying down time.

## What schools can do to promote play

Schools need to transmit a clear and strong message that parents who are able to share free time with their families and play with their children are being supportive, nurturing and productive. Such children will be poised for success, basking in the absolute and unconditional love of their parents and extended family. This love and attention is demonstrated by the fact that the parents are making the effort to be with their children, to listen, to talk and to enjoy their company. Schools should:

1 Consistently promote free play as an essential part of childhood.
2 Ensure children have adequate amounts of relaxation and play time built into the school day.
3 Discourage parents from overusing passive entertainment, such as television and computer games.
4 Emphasise that active play is the natural way to develop a healthy and fit body.
5 Emphasise the benefits of simple and cheap toys such as blocks and dolls, which children can use to develop their imagination.
6 Educate families about the increased resilience that will develop through free play and unscheduled activity time.
7 Suggest that, although well intentioned, shuttling children between numerous structured activities is probably not the best use of parent/child free time.
8 Advocate safe play spaces for children, perhaps by opening school fields or community facilities for the children and their parents to use after school, at weekends and during the school holidays.
9 Provide an appropriate academic schedule in school, balanced with interesting extra-curricular activity and free play time.
10 Stress the importance of the school's focus on the social and emotional developmental needs of the children as well as the academic.

According to Gray (2011): 'Restoring children's free play is not only the best gift we could give our children, it is also an essential gift if we want them to grow up to be psychologically healthy and emotionally competent adults.'

It is the responsibility of those who understand child development and are aware of the experiences necessary for children to develop into balanced and happy individuals to ensure that those in authority do not act in ignorance. Play is an essential part of childhood and cannot be replaced by formal education. To restrict children's opportunities to play would be to deprive them of a human right.

A third and equally important approach to enabling children to grow into well-balanced and contented adults would be the promotion of reading for pleasure. If all children could acquire the reading habit, lifelong learning could be ensured. Chapter 9 explores issues surrounding the development of reading in schools.

## References

Gray, P. (2011) The decline of play and the rise of psychopathology in children and adolescents. *American Journal of Play*, 3(4): 443–61.

Greenfield, S. (2011) Video games 'can alter children's brains'. *Daily Telegraph*, 14 November.

# Solution 3
## Promoting reading for pleasure

An increased focus on reading for pleasure in school will improve pupils' academic achievement, motivation, self-esteem and confidence. According to the Organisation for Economic Co-operation and Development: 'Reading for pleasure is the most important indicator of the future academic success of a child' (2002).

Reading is one of the main routes into learning and sixteen year olds who read for half an hour a day are on average one school year ahead of those who do not. Reading develops an individual's vocabulary, their general knowledge and their understanding of how texts are constructed. An increase in these skills will lead to a positive cycle of improvement, allowing the individual to read increasingly advanced material and further develop their vocabulary, general knowledge and understanding of texts.

Unfortunately, a significant number of pupils have inadequate reading skills. This will restrict their achievement in school and sap their confidence and motivation to learn. In 2013, one in seven of all Year 6 children left primary school without achieving the expected Level 4 in reading. At primary school, a child learns to read, but at secondary school the student needs to read in order to learn. These pupils will be at a huge disadvantage at the start of their secondary education.

A survey carried out by the National Literacy Trust in 2012 involving over 18,000 young people from eight to seventeen years of age revealed that: 'Pleasure in reading is closely related to an individual's reading competence and the enjoyment of reading declines steadily through the teenage years.'

Statistics from the Trust show that 16 per cent of adults in England (approximately 5.2 million people) could be described as being functionally illiterate, that is, their reading and writing skills are inadequate to cope with daily living and employment. Almost two-fifths (39 per cent) of Army recruits have reading ability below that of an average twelve year old. Poor literacy is a significant issue in prisons with 60 per cent of prisoners experiencing difficulty in basic literacy. The Trust estimates that 48 per cent of prisoners in the UK have a reading age below that of a Year 6 child.

However, reading is not only related to success in school. Research carried out by the charity 'The Reading Agency' reviewed fifty-one academic papers and reports published during the past ten years into the impact of reading on academic success and discovered a variety of additional non-academic benefits of reading for pleasure. 'There is strong evidence that reading for pleasure can increase empathy, improve relationships with others, reduce the symptoms of depression and the risk of dementia, and improve wellbeing throughout life' (Reading Agency 2015).

It has long been understood by the many groups and associations interested in the development of literacy skills that reading for pleasure has numerous benefits in addition to its essential role in maximising academic potential.

## Why reading for pleasure is important

### 1 Reading develops social and cultural empathy

Reading increases pupils' understanding of different cultures, groups and individuals within society. The pupil can read about situations that they will never experience personally. What life is like for people from different countries, cultures, religions, genders, age groups and social classes. What life was like during particular historical periods or may be like in the future. Children can anticipate what adult life might be like, read about places they would like to visit and hobbies or careers they might enjoy. Stories from alternative cultures may describe situations that are unfamiliar to the reader, but the emotions experienced by the characters will be the same. It will be enlightening for a teenage boy to read about a situation from a teenage girl's or a parent's point of view; for a victim to read about bullying from the bully's point of view; for a step-child to read about family relationships from a step-mother's point of view. Young people from materially comfortable backgrounds may learn to appreciate their own situation after reading stories that describe the hand-to-mouth existence of other children of their own age. Reading will open the pupil's eyes to the experiences, feelings and motivations of others, and an increased understanding of the reasons behind their behaviour will promote empathy between different individuals and groups.

## 2  Reading supports emotional development and provides security and reassurance

When sharing stories with young children, the reader can model sympathetic behaviour towards the characters and show how they are able to understand the concerns and worries of others.

> 'Oh poor Baby Bear, how horrible to have your chair broken like that. Poor little thing. Would you be upset if you were Baby Bear?'

> 'I think Ruby is probably jealous of the new baby and that is why she's hidden the baby's presents. I can remember your Mummy doing that when Auntie Rebecca was born.'

> 'I wonder if Jamie is being naughty because he's worried about starting school. Were you worried when you started school?'

Books can detail how others have coped with difficult life experiences: the death of a grandparent, a new baby in the family, a stay in hospital, unrequited love, life in a step-family or problems in school. A story can have the advantage of not appearing to preach, but presenting a situation and letting the reader consider options. Teenagers may be uncertain of how they feel about issues such as bullying, shyness, jealousy and anxiety. During reading, the individual can explore these issues without having to take sides or hold an opinion.

Texts that are obviously anti-bulling may not have the same effect as a book with several storylines, one of which explores bullying. Classical and traditional tales can be particularly useful in that the story is strong enough to have stood the test of time and, because the texts are set in a different context, they are less likely to seen by the reader as a sermon and more as a source of advice and guidance. Personal, Social, Health and Economic (PHSE) education programmes that focus on what not to do (don't smoke, drink alcohol, be a bully or take drugs) do not always have the same effect as a programme that tells pupils what to do instead. In the same way, younger children respond to positive messages: 'To stay safe, we always walk in the corridors at our school' rather than 'Don't run and knock each other over'.

## 3  Reading promotes creative thought

Reading stories stimulates creative thought, encouraging the imagination and promoting lateral thinking. Picture books can be art forms in their own right and present additional visual strands to a story, encouraging the child to read the story behind the words as a first step towards the development of inference. Separate stories can be followed through the illustrations and the text; this will replicate many situations in real life. Life is not straightforward and situations are not always as they appear initially.

Some books are understood to be make-believe, for example, fairy tales or science fiction, but other genres present possibilities. Would it be possible for animals to communicate with each other? Can the living communicate with ghosts?

Reading allows the individual to create situations from their imagination, the characters and settings being visualised by the reader. When watching TV programmes, the characters and context are created for the viewer.

## 4  Reading develops thinking skills

Reading promotes philosophical discussion. Themes within a story can stimulate moral debate and help pupils to see that situations are not always black and white but that there are shades of grey between.

Is it best to help others even when there is no personal advantage? Should you always tell the truth? Is stealing ever justified? Can you be cruel to be kind?

Reading will improve the reader's thinking skills. If you do not know about something, you cannot think or hold an opinion about it.

Reading will develop the individual's vocabulary, improving their ability to express themselves and structure their thoughts coherently, thereby enhancing their communication skills.

Books can be discussed with opinions aired and modified in the light of other readers' comments. It will become apparent to pupils that opinions are based on experience and beliefs and that an alternative interpretation of the 'truth' may be equally valid.

## 5 Reading provides entertainment

Reading can be relaxing and provide an escape from everyday life. Stories can be amusing enough for the reader to laugh out loud, making reading an enlightening and uplifting experience. If a pupil is worried or upset, they can lose themselves in another world and relax by getting involved in situations of their own choosing: a romantic or historical novel, a travel guide, an adventure or a horror or mystery story.

## 6 Reading improves general knowledge making the reader a more interesting person

A reader can learn more about every possible subject: the history of the local area, the geography of a holiday destination, how to deal with unruly pets, how to explore family history, the history of Chelsea FC, the Star Wars films, the development of the fashion industry or the roots of jazz. A pupil can become an expert on any topic of their choosing.

Through reading, the individual becomes a more interesting person, developing the ability to converse on a variety of topics with a wide range of people. Reading is a simple and cheap way to develop general knowledge and extend vocabulary, the essential components of good comprehension.

## 7  Reading develops self-efficacy

The ability to read to an adequate level is essential for a full and independent life, giving an individual access to the complete range of work and social opportunities. Without basic reading skills, an adult will experience problems with such routine tasks as taking a driving test, reading letters sent from school, perusing election leaflets, checking a prescription, applying for a job, reading safety notices or following a recipe.

Critical reading is necessary in order for the individual to maintain independence of thought and to differentiate between biased and unbiased information. Competent readers will be capable of developing balanced views, are more likely to vote and be less susceptible to manipulation and exploitation by others.

## Twenty top tips to encourage pupils to read for pleasure

1 Introduce pupils to authors or series of books that are popular with their age group. Sometimes pupils are unfamiliar with the texts their peers enjoy. Focus on those established authors that children are known to appreciate: Roald Dahl, James Patterson, J.K. Rowling, George R.R. Martin, Anne Fine, Jacqueline Wilson, Enid Blyton or Kate Atkinson.

2 Pupils may be interested in the lives of famous individuals and the biographies and autobiographies of political, musical, TV and sports personalities or famous historical figures may prove popular: Frank Lampard, Nelson Mandela, Amy Winehouse, Anne Frank, Mother Teresa, David Beckham, Winston Churchill, the Romans or Queen Victoria.

3 Joke, riddle, puzzle and quiz books provide alternative reading material. Try the 'Where's Wally' series, the Usborne puzzle adventures and general knowledge quiz books.

4 Reading newspaper articles about topics of interest will give reading a purpose. Pupils may like to read about art, music, sport, films, fashion, current affairs, recent films, TV programmes, big sporting events and music festivals.

5 There will be a magazine relating to every possible interest a pupil could have. Such material can be browsed through and dipped into, but doesn't require reading sequentially from beginning to end.

6 When a pupil lacks reading stamina, they may prefer short stories. Most children and teenagers enjoy Roald Dahl and Paul Jennings' collections or the short stories of Sherlock Holmes.

7 Comic books or Manga versions of English set texts will give pupils visual input to support their understanding of the text, as well as being an acceptable alternative in the eyes of their peers.

8 Poetry and rhyme have always been popular with pupils and the simplicity and rhythm of prose will be attractive to the less fluent, older reader.

9 Encourage alternative forms of reading using IT: iPads, books online, downloads, e-readers and audiobooks. Some students may perceive this sort of reading to be more adult. Reading on sites such as Wattpad encourages students to read and write. They can see the sort of issues that interest their peer group and that they like to write about, helping reading to become more personal.

10 Abridged versions of classics can be useful to provide an overview of the original texts read by the children during English lessons: Shakespeare, Austen, the Brontës or Dickens. Most of the larger publishing companies produce EAL (English as an Additional Language) versions of classics that have reduced and simplified text but are presented in an adult style.

11 Organise short courses to target specific aspects of pupils' reading skills: speed reading, comprehension, skimming, scanning and close reading. Offer such input to all pupils during PHSE or study skills lessons.

12 Try paired or shared reading. When an adult shares the reading of an interesting book, a pupil may be motivated enough to read on by themselves.

13 Reading sections of books relating to mainstream subjects can provide interesting perspectives to the topic, for example *The Diary of Ann Frank*, *Goodnight Mr Tom* or *The Boy in the Striped Pyjamas* will add a human dimension to World War II History modules.

If the child reader goes on a journey with the character, and takes them through those events in history, then I think they're more likely to be engaged with it.

(John Boyne, author of *The Boy in the Striped Pyjamas*)

14 Teach pupils that it is acceptable to pick up a book and not read past the first few pages if the book holds no intrinsic appeal. There is no point in a pupil ploughing on with something they are not enjoying.

15 Associations such as the United Kingdom Literacy Association, the Schools Library Association and the National Literacy Trust are an excellent source of resources and ideas for promoting reading across all age groups.

16 Always allow choice of material. *All* reading is good. It is unnecessary to direct the pupil towards 'worthy' material, but better to respect their preferences and start from their personal interests. Many pupils imagine fiction books to be the only 'proper' books. An introduction to other texts and confirmation of their importance as reading material can be a revelation: magazines, websites, eBooks, newspaper articles, poetry, manuals, graphic novels, short stories, comics and puzzle books would all fall into this category.

17 Use personal recommendation and have regular slots in Assemblies or Form Periods when members of staff or pupils read extracts or give short talks about books they have enjoyed.

18 Promote books. Mount displays of book recommendations, other work by the same author and books in the same genre or fiction and non-fiction material on the same topic. Advertise 'Good reads for artists/mathematicians/geographers/scientists'. Have displays of books in subject areas and corridors, entrance areas, main halls, the dining room and classrooms. Ensure the displays are changed on a regular basis.

19 Hold Readathons and sponsored reading events to support charities of the pupils' choice. Fundraising gives the more reluctant reader a valid reason to read. The reading material does not have to be seen as intellectually worthy because the emphasis is on raising money for charity. Pupils could record reading comics, magazines,

newspapers or easier books to younger siblings and children from lower year groups.

20 Create a school website with personal recommendations, books of topical interest, books that are in the news at the moment, suggestions for books to be read by the time you are fourteen, sixteen or eighteen and 'If you liked this, you'll love this …' promotions.

Reading for pleasure, participating in sport and enjoying free play are three activities that schools could use to promote children's well-being and would provide suitable educational targets for any establishment striving to improve the holistic development of all the children in their care.

## References

Festival of Politics (2012) *The Importance of Reading to Children and to Society*. London: Reading Agency.

Literacy Changes Lives (2014) 'How reading can help children escape poverty' by the Read On. Get On. Association, London. *A New Perspective on Health, Employment and Crime*. London: Literacy Trust.

Organisation for Economic Co-operation and Development (2002) *Literacy skills for the world of tomorrow*. Paris: OECD.

The Reading Agency (2015) Literature Review: The impact of reading for pleasure and empowerment, June. The review was funded by BOP Consulting.

# Ten top tips and advice sheets

# Advice sheets

This chapter compromises ten advice sheets designed to support both pupil and teacher. The sheets can be adapted as appropriate to pupils' need, age and level of development.

The 'Active learning', 'The brain and learning', 'Listening skills', 'Organisation', 'Specific Learning Differences' and 'Resilience' sheets each give teachers ten useful strategies to support these aspects of pupil metacognition.

The 'Healthy lifestyle' and 'Motivation' sheets, and 'How I learn' and 'Study skills' questionnaires are designed as pupil advice sheets, and could be used for discussion within a Study Skill or PHSE programme.

Each advice sheet is presented on new page for ease of photocopying.

# Active learning techniques

Learning is most effective when pupils do something with the information.

1 *Concept mapping*

Pupils work in pairs or small groups with sets of concept cards to put into an order. For example, give pupils five concept cards: carbon in air, carbon in bacteria and fungi, carbon in organic molecules in animals, coal/oil/gas, and carbon in organic molecules in plants. The pupils order the cards by creating a map around them using such links as respiration, photosynthesis and combustion.

2 *Role play*

This can be a popular activity with pupils. It is seen as fun and everyone can be actively involved. Small group or paired work will ensure that everyone is able to participate. A good example of a popular role play activity would be 'Hot Seating', when a volunteer takes on the role of a historical personality, a scientist, a politician, a religious or literary figure and the rest of the class ask the volunteer questions about their life, behaviour, work or beliefs.

3 *'Pass the problem'*

The pupils devise problems based on recently completed work for partners or other group members to solve.

4 *Board and card games*

There are numerous board and card games that are easily adapted for use in the classroom, for example Snap, Snakes and Ladders, Happy Families, Old Maid, Dominoes and Bingo. Spend a lesson making games with pupils working individually, in pairs or in small groups to design a board or card game for their peers to play. They will learn as they discuss the information, think of suitably challenging questions and how the information links together.

5 *Answer and pass Dominoes*

Each pupil has a card with a question and an answer on it. One pupil reads out the question and the pupil who thinks they have the correct answer on their card responds. If they are correct, they read out their question, another pupil provides what they think to be the correct answer and so on. Pupils or adults can make the sets of cards. The activity can be timed to increase pupil focus.

## Active learning techniques *continued*

### 6 *Adapt TV games*

Blockbusters would be one example of a TV gameshow that could be adapted for classroom use. One-half of the class could work vertically and one-half horizontally across the grid. Questions can be set for any subject and at any level. What 'D' did John Fisher invent in 1904? Which 'S' is the city where Francis Ferdinand was shot? The first team to cross the grid wins. Another example of an easily adaptable TV game would be 'A Question of Sport'. This game could be adapted to any subject, with questions set at different levels as appropriate for the competing teams.

### 7 *Peer testing*

Flash cards can be used in a variety of ways to test vocabulary, formulae, spelling, dates, definitions or names. Work individually, in pairs or in small groups. Timing pupils' responses will add a competitive element if required. How many questions can be answered correctly in one minute?

### 8 *Sabotage*

One pair or group delivers a summary of a previous lesson, topic or module with an agreed number of deliberate errors for the rest of the class to identify.

### 9 *Hierarchy cards*

The class is presented with cards covering, for example, all the arguments for dropping an atomic bomb on Japan in 1945. The pupils discuss the arguments within small groups and then put the cards in order of importance.

### 10 *Snowball techniques*

Pupils work in pairs to discuss a topic and devise two important questions or key points for further discussion. Each pair joins with another pair and chooses the best question or key point. The group then discusses their point with another group. This technique ensures everyone is able to participate.

## The brain and learning

1 *The brain appreciates the repetition of information*

The more an activity is practised or information revised, the stronger related links in the brain will become. Practice and repetition are an essential part of learning and securing knowledge.

2 *The brain works by making links*

In order to make sense of information, the brain will connect new information to what is already known. The more related information it is exposed to, the more links made and the deeper the learning. Reading around a subject and discussing topics will help the brain to organise information and create patterns and clusters of facts and ideas.

3 *Try to vary the ways in which learning occurs*

The brain enjoys variety, challenge and working out difficult problems. The unusual will be more memorable than the mundane.

4 *Keep learning active*

The brain learns best when it has to think about and do something with the information, perhaps changing text into a visual display: comic strips, diagrams, charts or a timeline.

5 *Pay attention in order to learn*

Reduce distractions: attention is the key to memorising. By making a decision to focus on something, the information is given personal meaning and becomes easier to recall.

6 *The brain will work effectively when the body's physical and mental needs are met*

It is difficult to learn effectively when distracted, tired, anxious, uncomfortable or hungry.

7 *Take regular exercise*

The brain needs a good supply of oxygen. When physical activity takes place, the brain will receive the best supply of oxygenated blood.

## The brain and learning *continued*

8 *A good diet is required for effective learning*

Eat regularly and don't skip meals. The brain uses 20 per cent of the body's food intake and will perform less well when its energy supply drops. A student's test results will be lower when they haven't eaten.

9 *Stress impacts on brain function*

Devise personal strategies to reduce anxiety – see the pupil advice sheet for a healthy lifestyle. Stress uses up working memory, leaving less capacity available for the brain to process and encode new information. When worried or anxious, energy will be diverted from the brain to the limbs to prepare the individual for flight from the perceived threat.

10 *Sleep is vital*

Sleep plays a critical role in the consolidation of information. Sleep is the time when the brain is able to order recent input and create long-term memories.

# Developing pupils' listening and attention skills

1 *Physical comfort*

For a pupil's attention to be maximised, they will need to be physically comfortable, sitting in a suitable chair, with a good view of what is happening in the classroom. The room should be adequately ventilated and lit, not over noisy and with enough personal space for each child.

2 *Vary input*

For pupils who are easily distracted, regular changes of activity will help them to refocus. If the adult can see that several pupils are beginning to fidget, having a movement break where all the children can get out of their seats and stretch, may be enough for most pupils to re-settle.

3 *Cut back on teacher talk*

Keep teacher talk to a minimum and alternate periods of instruction with practical activity or opportunity for pupil discussion.

4 *Check pupils' ability to multi-task*

Reduce the need for pupil multi-tasking. Many children find it difficult to listen to information and take notes. They may be distracted by trying to write neatly or write quickly, spell accurately or decide what is worth recording. It may be more effective for them to listen, understand and then make notes.

5 *Allow controlled fidgeting*

Let pupils doodle or fidget as long as they don't disturb other children. Many children cannot listen properly when they have to concentrate on keeping still. Allowing the pupil to fiddle with a small piece of blu-tack or paper clip will not disturb other children, yet give the fidget something to do with their hands. Stretching their legs or feet about under the table will provide additional opportunities to move without disturbing others.

6 *Give recognition as appropriate*

Give appropriate praise or encouragement when pupils are paying attention and trying to listen.

## Developing pupils' listening and attention skills *continued*

7 *Use pupils for monitoring*

When pupils are working in pairs, they can monitor each other's attention and reinforce understanding. To check pupils have understood, ask one child to repeat the instructions to their group or partner.

8 *Draw attention to important points*

To draw pupils' attention to important information, emphasise any key points. 'Now, it is really important that you understand this.' 'You will need to know this, so listen carefully.' 'Attention everyone, this next bit is important.'

9 *Use visual aids*

Support verbal input with visual aids to help understanding or fill gaps when attention has flagged. If instructions are listed on the whiteboard, pupils can refer back to them to ensure they are still on the right track even when they have drifted away for a few moments.

10 *Know the individual*

It is worth trying to ascertain why pupils have a concentration problem. Do they process language slowly and information is being given too quickly for them to assimilate? Do they have adequate experience of listening and paying attention, or is it a specific skill that needs development? Do they have an underlying language weakness and are unable to follow what is being said? Do they have a hearing difficulty? Sometimes a minor adjustment in teaching approach can improve a pupil's attention span dramatically.

## Organisation: how to help pupils to organise themselves

1 *Model good practice*

   Demonstrate your own methods for organisation: noting dates in a diary, keeping lists to prioritise tasks, keeping your desk tidy, carrying spare equipment and making brief plans for written work. If pupils are disorganised, their family are probably disorganised and they may not be aware of how to help themselves.

2 *Timetables*

   Give the pupil photocopied timetables to keep in different places: on their bedroom wall, in their desk and in the front of their school bag.

3 *Organise homework*

   Ensure pupils record homework immediately and note down any deadlines for work or tests that will require revision.

4 *Extol the virtues of a routine*

   Explain the benefits of keeping to routines (as suitable for the age of the child): after school club or activity, walk home, something to eat, thirty minutes TV, homework, evening meal, homework, shower and bed.

5 *Encourage a little and often approach*

   Regular study sessions are of more benefit than occasional bursts of intense effort to keep on top of a workload. If a pupil knows they have done their allotted amount of work, they can enjoy their free time without feeling guilty.

6 *Promote automatic behaviour*

   Encourage an automatic approach to organisation. Files are always kept either in the pupil's locker or their bag. At the end of each lesson, the pupil routinely packs their belongings into their school bag. If they are distracted and talking to friends, they will still pack their belongings into their bag because that is their usual routine. Purse or wallet always in inside pocket of jacket. Pens always returned to pencil case. Phone always zipped in top inside pocket of jacket. Point out the advantage of keeping spare sets of equipment: spare pens in the front of their school bag, an extra set of Maths equipment on a shelf in their bedroom and spare hockey socks in their locker.

# Organisation: how to help pupils to organise themselves

*continued*

7 *Use IT*

Encourage the use of IT for planning work: keeping a reminder on their phone for the dates of drama rehearsals, the time of a football match, coursework deadlines or recording exam timetables.

8 *Social contacts*

Encourage the pupils to keep the numbers of reliable peers on their phones in case they need to check homework, the time of a match or content of a test.

9 *Do spot checks in lessons*

Check a few pupils' files every week. Demonstrate the use of dividers, colour coding, how to create an index and file handouts to keep work in a good order. Impress on the pupils that neat files make learning easier.

10 *Make good use of lists*

Show the pupil how to keep lists as a running record to aid memory. Each evening they can look at the list, cross off what they have done, remind themselves of any outstanding commitments and then pack their school bag for the following day.

## Specific learning difficulties or differences

1  Specific Learning Difficulty (SpLD) is an umbrella term covering such conditions as dyslexia, dyspraxia, dyscalculia and attention deficit disorders in addition to aspects of autism and language difficulties.

2  SpLDs differ from General Learning Difficulties in that the pupil will have strengths and weaknesses, rather than a weakness across the board.

3  For many children, a diagnosis will depend on when and by whom they are assessed. A pre-school child may be diagnosed as experiencing a language and communication problem, the same child as having a literacy difficulty when they are in primary school and, if their needs are not met, an emotional or behavioural problem in secondary school. A child may be diagnosed as dyspraxic by an occupational therapist, language impaired by a speech therapist, visually impaired by an optometrist or dyslexic by an educational psychologist.

4  There is always an overlap of symptoms in SpLDs. Poor concentration, slow processing or a weak memory may present the child with a difficulty, but the root cause in each individual may be different.

5  The degree to which a pupil is affected by any weaknesses will depend upon their personal strengths and the context of their situation. The pupil may be diagnosed as severely dyslexic but be quick witted, highly motivated, hard working, have an ability in Music, ICT, PE, Drama or Design, have good social skills, be popular with their peers, receive sympathetic support from their family and have developed a resilient personality. Such pupils may go through school feeling a little irritated by their inability to spell accurately, learn French vocabulary or process information quickly, but their overall achievement need not be affected.

6  The level of a pupil's self-esteem will affect their performance. They will be capable of what they believe they are capable.

7   Those pupils who succeed at school tend to be logical, sequential thinkers, good auditory learners, be able to maintain concentration without too much effort, have neat presentation skills and content to conform and behave. Many pupils will be the exact opposite of this, but this does not necessarily mean they have a specific learning difficulty.

8   For many pupils the school situation creates problems. A limited attention span may be seen as a disability in a forty-minute lesson, but as an asset in a work situation where having the skill to be able to juggle several activities simultaneously, initiate projects and move rapidly from one task to another will be seen as a distinct advantage. Constantly out of their seat or possessing boundless energy? Deviating from class activity or independent of thought? Poor social skills and a bossy attitude or holding passionate opinions and leadership skills? Poor organisation or thoughtful and absorbed in their own creativity?

9   A diagnosis of a SpLD should not be seen as an excuse for the pupil to underperform, but a reason for adults in school to review their teaching methods.

10  Pupils should be constantly reminded that strategies exist to circumvent all problems.

## Resilience: developing pupils' resilience

An individual's resilience relates to their ability to recover from adversity. Although pupils' levels of resilience will be influenced by many factors from home background to individual personality, there are ways to increase a pupil's ability to bounce back from difficulties and manage stressful situations.

1 *Provide resilient role models*

   Family, teachers, famous personalities and other pupils. Discuss how they have dealt with challenging circumstances.

2 *Teach the pupils the importance of keeping healthy and point out the links between physical and mental health*

   Pupils should eat properly, exercise and allow enough time for relaxation.

3 *Encourage pupils to set themselves reasonable goals*

   Focus on what has been accomplished rather than on what hasn't. Break down larger assignments and take a 'one small step at a time' approach to problem solving. Help the pupils to see testing times as an opportunity to demonstrate their strength of character.

4 *Help pupils manage social conflict and repair relationships*

   Show them how to be kind and make allowances for friends without becoming a doormat.

5 *Allow pupils to make decisions*

   Making decisions about situations that directly affect them will help to develop independence.

6 *When pupils face challenging situations, help them to look at the problem in the broader context and keep a long-term perspective*

   There will be a future beyond the current situation and that future can be good. An optimistic outlook enables children to see the good things in life and persevere.

## Resilience: developing pupils' resilience *continued*

7 *Remind pupils of ways they have dealt with problems in the past*

Help them realise that these past challenges have helped develop the strength required to handle future difficulties.

8 *Encourage pupils to see the humour in life*

Help them be able to laugh at themselves.

9 *Remind pupils of their successes*

Look at achievements they can be proud of and the steps they have already taken to improve. Worrying can affect learning and performance, but when children feel confident they will be less likely to panic or make silly mistakes.

10 *Teach pupils to listen to and empathise with others and to maintain wide social networks*

Mixing with friends and acquaintances will provide social support and strengthen resilience.

## A healthy lifestyle

1 *Take exercise*

Exercise doesn't have to be extreme; a walk or a bike ride in the fresh air will give you a break, time to think things over, relax and appreciate your surroundings.

2 *Join a sports club or team*

Playing sport will be of benefit because it will involve social contact, physical activity and time spent away from the daily routine.

3 *Have a social life*

The company of others will promote personal happiness, giving opportunities to enjoy shared interests, offer support, discuss concerns, put worries into perspective or just take a break from work.

4 *Get enough sleep*

Adequate sleep is essential for good mental and physical health. To get to sleep, have a warm bath or a shower, make sure the room is dark, draw your curtains and switch off any laptops, computers or phone screens. It is easy to worry at night because there are fewer distractions from troubling thoughts, so write down anything that is a concern and then dismiss it from your mind to think about in the morning. Keeping a regular bedtime helps; it is easier to fall asleep when sleeping habits are well established.

5 *Develop any personal hobbies or interests*

Go shopping, to the cinema or a friend's house. Interests outside school help with relaxation and keep a balance in your life. Everyone will enjoy different sorts of activities: attending a church group, being a member of a local drama club or choir, babysitting younger children, playing in a local band or having a Saturday job. Developing alternative talents will help you to keep school life in perspective.

## A healthy lifestyle *continued*

6 *Get out in the fresh air*

Walking or cycling to and from school will give you a break from centrally heated homes and stuffy classrooms. Walking increases oxygen supplies to the brain and helps it to work more effectively.

7 *Eat well*

You need to eat adequate amounts of food. If you eat too much sugary food, your energy levels will fluctuate and make it more difficult to concentrate. Try to avoid fizzy drinks or anything with too much added sugar.

8 *Be kind to yourself*

When setting yourself challenges, make them realistic. Take a small-step approach and you will be less likely to be disappointed or give up.

9 *Ask for help from others*

Don't be too proud to ask for help. Everyone likes to feel useful, so you will be helping others to feel good about themselves. There may be a time in the future when you will be able to return favours.

10 *Use social networking sites sensibly*

Social networking sites are not real life. Not everyone is having a wonderful time, always going out with friends, happy or feeling great about the way they look. Live in the real world.

## How to motivate yourself

1 *Manage your environment*

   Listen to music to put you in the correct frame of mind: relaxed and calm or motivated and ready to take on a challenge.

2 *Surround yourself with pleasant and positive people*

   Talk to supportive family and friends who will be kind and boost your confidence.

3 *Manage any unsettling thoughts*

   Visualise what it will be like to finish a task, succeed at the challenge you have been set, manage the demands made of you and receive positive feedback.

4 *Know how you work and play to your strengths*

   Challenges will motivate those individuals who enjoy change and exploring the unknown, while others prefer security and will be motivated by maintaining the status quo.

5 *When you have doubts, remind yourself of previous successes*

   Think of things that you have done well, and tell yourself that, as you have succeeded before, it is quite possible to do it again.

6 *Establish short-term and long-term goals*

   You can take a small-step approach while still being aware of your ultimate aims. Give yourself rewards and incentives along the way. 'When I have managed a week of work experience, I'll buy myself that new pair of shoes/cinema tickets/CD.'

7 *If you are procrastinating, make a short-term deal with yourself*

   If I write out this essay/tidy my bedroom/read this chapter, then I can watch EastEnders/have a bath/eat a packet of crisps.

8 *Pretend to be motivated*

   When people assume that you are motivated, they will be supportive and enthusiastic too, which may be enough to galvanise you into action.

## How to motivate yourself *continued*

9 *Look after yourself and maintain a healthy lifestyle*

   When you are physically fit, you will be mentally alert. Take adequate amounts of exercise, eat a balanced diet and make sure you get enough sleep. If you feel things are getting too much, do something that you know will help you to relax: have a bath, watch a DVD, go for a swim, take the dog for a walk or meet up with friends.

10 *Monitor your performance*

   Write out a list of tasks and tick each one off when completed. This will provide evidence of your progress.

## Questionnaire: how I learn

This questionnaire could be used as a discussion tool to increase pupil awareness of their learning styles and preferences or as a starting point for pastoral staff in a PHSE lesson. Teaching staff could use pupil feedback from the questionnaire to inform future lesson planning.

1 What do you enjoy most about school/outside school?

   Any sort of sport. I play for school and club hockey teams. I quite like Biology and English this year because I like the teachers and they seem to like me.

2 What do you dislike most about school/outside school?

   I find it hard to revise for exams. I'm quite good in class, but don't seem to be able to get my ideas down on paper clearly or quickly enough. It's a shame because I need five good GCSEs to get into college and I'm not sure I'll be able to get them.

3 How would you describe your favourite teachers? What aspect of their teaching do you most appreciate?

   I like teachers who let you ask questions without getting cross, teachers who don't have favourites but seem interested in everyone. They have a bit of a sense of humour but can keep control of the class too. A relaxed but fairly quiet atmosphere helps me to learn.

4 What type of lessons do you not enjoy or learn from?

   I find it hard to concentrate when teachers just talk for a long time and you have to sit quietly and listen. They won't let you ask questions. They'll say they've already told you something but they haven't.

5 What kind of pupils do you like spending time with?

   Sporty ones who work hard but can be fun as well. They are kind and will help if you don't understand something. Good friends who don't talk behind your back.

6 What do you like most about yourself?

   I think I am a good friend. I'm reliable and don't let people down. I'm basically a kind and caring person and people like me.

## Questionnaire: how I learn *continued*

7 Is there anything you would like to change about yourself?

I wish I could do better in tests and exams.

8 What characteristics do you possess that your teachers, friends or parents might not know about?

I don't know. Maybe my teachers don't realise how hard I try in school. I think my parents do though.

9 Do you know how you learn best?

I like doing practical things to help me understand how everything fits together. I like it when the teacher talks about every day examples, so you can see how a theory applies in the real world. Going over stuff until it is straight in my head helps too, really clear and simple until I understand and then getting more difficult after that.

10 If you were to design a new school with different methods of teaching, what would it be like?

I'd have a lot more sport, some type of sport every day. It would help me to concentrate in lessons if I knew I had a Games or PE lesson next. I like playing in matches but I'm not always chosen for teams. If we did more sport, we could have more teams and everyone could get a game.

# Questionnaire: study skills

## 1 Reading

Do you read for pleasure?

What sort of reading material do you choose?

When reading silently, do you read word for word?

Would you use different reading techniques in different situations?

Do you have enough time to complete reading tasks set in class or for homework?

## 2 Memory

What techniques do you use when revising for tests and exams?

Can you remember modern foreign language vocabulary and scientific and mathematical formulae easily?

Can you remember sequences easily, for example, the stages of solving a mathematical problem?

## 3 Attention

Can you concentrate throughout a lesson or does your attention wander?

If you do have a problem with concentration, what do you do?

Do you always participate fully in lessons?

When you are asked a question or to repeat instructions, are you always able to remember what has been said?

## Questionnaire: study skills *continued*

4 *Organisation*

Do you regularly forget or lose equipment, homework and sports kit?

Is your desk/bedroom/locker/school bag so untidy that you are unable to find your belongings?

5 *Note taking*

Can you always pick out the important facts from information?

How do you take notes?

Can you make notes and listen at the same time?

6 *Essays*

Do you always understand what an essay title is asking you to do?

Do you have a problem with planning essays? Do you know what to include and what to leave out?

Do you have a good grasp of basic grammar and punctuation?

Are you aware of the strengths and weaknesses that teachers identify regularly in your essays?

7 *Spelling*

Has spelling ever been a problem for you?

Do you have to use spellcheckers?

Can you proofread accurately?

## Questionnaire: study skills *continued*

8 *Presentation of work*

Is your handwriting legible?

Are your diagrams and maps neat and easy to interpret?

Can you write quickly enough to complete tasks within the allotted time?

Are you often disappointed with the appearance of your work?

Do you try your best to be neat but your work is still untidy?

9 *Exams and revision*

Do you find revision difficult?

What aspect do you find most difficult?

Are the grades you get for exams similar to the grades you get for your coursework?

Do your exam results reflect the effort you make to revise?

Do you get unduly anxious about the exams themselves?

10 *Group work and oral presentations*

Are you able to give confident oral presentations?

Can you work as a member of a group?

Do you enjoy group work?

# Index